Congratu

Hope you ~

(and reviewing

my book!

This is What
PERFECT
Looks Like

This is What PERFECT Looks Like

A Memoir

HEATHER HOUSE

PREFACE

As we emerged from the blur of the first year of life with twins, I began to reflect on how profoundly I was changed by the experience of being Fern's mom. I started journaling at night, telling myself the stories I wanted to remember. Then I noticed I couldn't go anywhere without a pen and pad of paper for fear I would recall a story and not have a place to write it down. Pretty soon I had a file full of scraps of paper and several hundred pages of typed memories. As I was organizing them one day, I realized I was no longer just journaling for myself. I was writing a book. And I look forward to the day when Fern and I read and discuss this book together.

By no means is this a complete account of the first three years of Fern's life. I left out a lot of the boring stuff. I also left out some of the interesting stuff out. Like how much Fern enjoyed receiving reiki and cranial sacral treatments. And how she learned to love the water. And trampolines.

My understanding of the events that took place over the last three years is changing as I change as a person. Thank you for reading this book, and thank you for understanding that, like me, all of these stories are still works in progress.

ACKNOWLEDGMENTS

First and foremost, I want to thank Fern. You are more than just a muse. You are my daughter and I love you dearly.

I would like to thank my husband Will who, for almost two years straight, put up with the tap tap tapping sounds of a keyboard every night before bedtime as I typed out this story. Your feedback kept me honest, your encouragement kept me going and your love still makes my heart spark.

I would also like to thank Beth, Devon, Rebecca and Carolyn for forming a writers' group at exactly the right time in my life. You helped me cut through my bullshit and be a better writer.

Thank you to Monica for accepting the writing challenge and reading some of my worst writing.

Thank you Michele, Kevin, Jennifer and Matt for the writer's retreat hospitality.

And thank you Cara, for knowing exactly how to be my best friend and for helping me seem nicer on paper than I am in real life.

Thank you to my editor, Melissa Thorpe Dalton, for the final polish.

I would also like to thank all the friends and family members who have supported us on this journey. You brought us food, visited us in the hospital, cared for the boys, gave us hugs, sent encouraging messages, shared your own stories and, most generously, listened to ours.

Thank you to all the medical professionals, midwives, conventional and alternative healers, teachers, therapists and aides who have helped Fern on this journey so far. You saved us. You believed in us and you cheered us on. You set high expectations and it has been a joy to watch Fern rise to meet them.

And finally, a word for Sylvan and Cypress. You boys are the center of my world and I love you more than life itself. For every time Fern caused me to question who I was, you were there reaffirming my place in this world. But you are little and you wonder why I haven't written a book about you. When I asked what I should write about you, Cypress suggested I could tell the story about how he got the scar on his forehead. And Sylvan thought there was probably a chapter or two about the new shoes he got last week. One day I think you'll appreciate the simple fact that when love comes easily, there's not enough material to fill a book.

For Sylvan and Cypress,
Fern's first and best teachers.

ONE

The News I'd Been Dreading

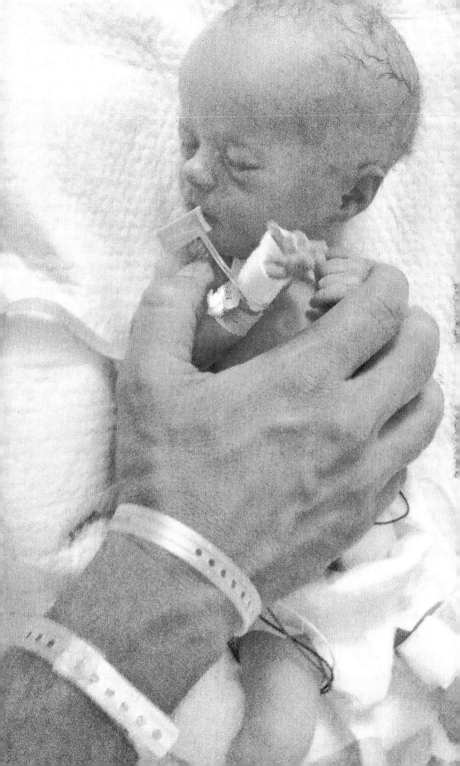

"Ms. House? I'm Dr. Smith."

Finally. I've waited all night and all morning to meet this woman. She's come with the absurdly pretty resident who was called to pacify me at 3 A.M., and another resident I'm meeting for the first time.

Dr. Smith looked pointedly at my friends sitting on the couch. "I'd like to talk with you and your husband privately. Do you want anyone to leave?"

I turned to Theresa and Midwife Lucy, who both looked pretty tired. They smiled encouragingly and offered to leave if that's what I wanted.

"No, thank you. I want them to stay," I answered.

"Okay," Dr. Smith said briskly. "I hear you have concerns about your daughter having Down syndrome."

I hate the way I feel around doctors, especially when I'm wearing a hospital gown and have bags under my eyes.

I nodded.

Dr. Smith nodded back. "I share your concerns."

And there it was. The news I'd been dreading since I'd first laid eyes on my daughter twelve hours prior.

"Okay," I said, not crying yet. That would come later. For the moment, I was pragmatic. Doctors are busy people and I figured I'd better hold it together so she could tell me the plan that was going to make this all better before she had to rush off to the next patient.

Dr. Smith talked fast, almost excitedly, and the too-pretty resident nodded in agreement.

"....can't say 100% until the blood work comes back, but the markers are there..."

I wonder if she golfs. She definitely gets her hair highlighted by a professional, someone good. Probably someone she has been seeing for years.

"......and you're going to love her just like your other children..."

She must have busted her ass to get this job. Head of the Neonatal Intensive Care Unit? Yeah, she's worked hard. I wonder if she's paid off her car yet.

"....and they're even in commercials now..."

She's pretty and athletic. I bet she even has a happy marriage. But why is she wearing ugly shoes? They don't even look comfortable for standing on this hard floor all day.

"...so we'll run some tests and Dr. Burn will be by to check her heart later...."

Is she always this cheerful? She sure does have a lot of energy. I wonder if she has kids. What's it like to be the child of a doctor? I wish I was smarter.

Dr. Smith was looking at me. "Do you have any questions for me?"

"Um....," I turned to my husband. "Will?"

I don't remember what we asked her. We probably went into survival mode, which is something Will and I are pretty good at when we don't know what else to do. Once, before we had kids, we got lost while canoeing in the Everglades. We stood in our canoe and could see nothing but miles and miles of waving grass. It would have been the perfect time to freak out, but we didn't. Instead, we went into survival mode:

Step 1: Safety first. Check for alligators and pythons.

Step 2: Remove barriers to clear thinking. Drink water, reapply sunblock and eat a candy bar.

Step 3: Come up with a plan. We could try to retrace our canoe path through the sea of grass, never mind the fact that the water is quickly receding and everything looks completely different than it did just five minutes ago.

Step 4: Act quickly. Or we will soon be stuck here.

Step 5: Scratch that. Better move slowly. Slow mistakes are small mistakes.

There we were, lost again, but this time right in the middle of Clarkesville, PA. We probably asked Dr. Smith for information about the NICU. Or asked her when we could get out of the hospital. Mostly I just remember nodding, trying to hold it together, waiting for the plan that was going to make everything alright.

Dr. Smith reassured us that Fern was "super cute" and, after giving us a brief update on Fern's health and preparing us for the likelihood of a two-week stint in the NICU, she and her entourage left the room, taking with them the plan for how they were going to make this all better.

As the door shut behind her, I turned to Will and our friends.

"FUUUUUUUUCK!" I wailed.

The flood gates opened. Tears poured out and reality rushed in, creating a dangerous undertow threatening to pull me under. I sobbed and gasped for breath.

Sobbing. Such an interesting word when used to describe the tears flowing from a grown woman. Until you've actually sobbed. It's easy to confuse sobbing with crying. Yet, crying carries with it a modicum of dignity, has an almost pretty quality on the right girl. When someone is said to be crying, you get the sense that some part of them is still intact, perhaps even a little bit happy. Able to see the forest for the trees. One can have a good cry, feign a little smile and say something like, "Well at least I'm better off without him."

In order to truly sob, one has to feel like everything has been lost. Sobbing is shattered mourning dreams. Sobbing is what you do when life has veered wildly off-course, steering you into a chasm of despair. Sobbing is the frustration of the unfairness of life wet on your cheeks, robbing you of breath, reason, and hope.

And boy did I sob.

The only thing better than sobbing is sobbing with a healthy side serving of ranting and cursing.

"I don't want this! This is not the life I want!!" I wailed. "This is not how it's supposed to be! Why me??? FUCKSHIT-GODDAMNIT! I don't want to be in the Mother-of-a-Retard club. I just want my old life back. I don't care if I CAN do this, I don't WANT TO! What if I have to hold her hand to cross the street when she's 20!? She's never going to get married! The Special Olympics aren't even real sports! No NO NO NOOO!!!!"

It would days before I asked what having Down syndrome meant for Fern.

It was all about *me* and what Down syndrome was doing to mess up MY life.

Poor Fern. Not even 4 pounds yet, alone in the NICU while her mama is all broke down feeling sorry for herself in room 201.

•   •   •

It had been a long night. The twins were born via cesarean at 8:15 P.M. and 8:17 P.M. I didn't get to touch Fern, much less hold her, in the operating room. After some preliminary examinations, she was whisked away to the NICU. When the c-section was complete, Sylvan was bundled and put into my arms like a consolation prize so we could ride back to our room together.

Will did his best to be in two places at once. When he was with Fern, I wanted him in the room with me. When he was in the room with me and Sylvan, it meant Fern was alone in the NICU. And I hated to think of that. We have no family in the area, so the NICU staff agreed that Theresa and Lucy could be part of our family for the duration of our stay.

To know Theresa is to know the meaning of calm, loving and gentle. Knowing Theresa sat by Fern's side, stroking her little head while I stayed in my room for the mandatory hour of observation in post-op recovery, helped me relax. Midwife Lucy stayed with me to help get Sylvan nursing and Will was free to move between rooms as he liked.

After a bit, Theresa came back to my room with a report. "Fern is very alert. And she seems really eager to meet her mama. She keeps thrusting her tongue, like she's ready to nurse."

Even then, a tiny red flag went up in my head. Babies don't normally thrust their tongue when they are hungry, do they?

My legs were still numb from the epidural when I finally got the thumbs up to meet Fern. Sylvan was not allowed in the NICU so long as he was a patient of the hospital, so I handed him to Will. Then Theresa and Midwife Lucy followed as the nurse wheeled my bed the short distance from my room to the NICU. NICU nurses cleared a wide path for my bed and I was parked alongside Fern's warming table. There she was. Skinny. Dazed. Alien. I reached into the warming bed to touch my daughter, calling her by the name I'd given her when she was just a tiny embryo.

"Hi Fern."

I turned to Theresa and Midwife Lucy. "She's so tiny. How is it she's so tiny?"

I never dreamed I'd give birth to a 3lb 14oz baby. I knew it was possible my twins would be on the smaller side, but I'd held cantaloupes bigger than this baby. Even when we took into account the margin of error for ultrasound measurements, we never expected Fern to weigh less than 4 pounds.

"It looks like she has Down syndrome." I said matter-of-factly. I'd never actually seen a 3lb 14oz baby with Down syndrome, but, to me, Fern looked like the poster child.

"No," Midwife Lucy assured me. "Premies are just kind of different looking. She just needs to gain some weight."

Lucy is a gifted midwife. She had given me the miraculous, almost mystical, homebirth of my first child, Cypress, who we named in homage to our two backcountry canoe trips through the Everglades. She knew I would be disappointed about delivering the twins via c-section, so she drove 80 minutes to the hospital to offer whatever support she could as friend, midwife and lactation consultant. She had experience with perhaps hundreds of newborns. Midwife Lucy was humble and forthright, and I trusted her opinion. But I had a mother's nagging hunch that something wasn't quite right about Fern.

A nursed passed by.

"Excuse me," I called out. "Does my baby have Down syndrome?"

The nurse approached cautiously. "I don't know. I'll have to get someone to answer that for you. Would you like to hold her?"

Then Fern was in my arms. As I did with Sylvan, I offered Fern my breast immediately. Unlike Sylvan, who started sucking vigorously as soon as the nipple made contact with his lips, Fern looked at me with curious eyes, but she did not latch. Midwife Lucy helped me with positioning and tickled Fern's cheek to stimulate some sucking. Her response was weak. We tried the other breast with the same result.

"She's so tiny," I repeated. "How did I ever make such a tiny baby?" I never imagined such a tiny baby could come out of my 5'10" body.

I turned to Midwife Lucy. "You really don't think she has Down syndrome?"

"No, no. Look!" she said. "Her ears are at a normal height, they're a normal size. And she doesn't have a crease across her palm. She's fine. She's just small."

I desperately wanted to believe her. I wanted the nagging hunch to be wrong, misplaced. I wanted it to be nothing more that the ghost of a prenatal fear long presumed dead come back to haunt me.

Suddenly, I vomited the cranberry juice I drank in post-op recovery all over Fern. As Theresa and Lucy scrambled to find towels and a bucket, I wiped the pinkish vomit from Fern's face.

Nice to meet you, baby girl.

Then it was time to go back to my room, where Will and Sylvan were waiting for me.

Over the next couple of hours, the effects of the epidural wore off and my entire body shook uncontrollably. I was simultaneously freezing in some places and burning up in others. I regained feeling in my legs and was able to keep a little food down. Things were quieting down and Midwife Lucy left with the promise to return the next day. Before we turned in for the night, Theresa offered to take me in a wheelchair to the NICU one more time.

We looked at Fern laying wide awake on the warming table taking in the midnight lights and sounds of the surprisingly peaceful NICU.

"She's so tiny, Theresa. Do you think she has Down syndrome?"

Theresa shrugged, "I don't really know. She's really beautiful, Heather. She's so peaceful."

I looked at my baby and did not find her beautiful. She did seem peaceful, but something was not right.

"Excuse me, Nurse!" I blurted at a woman passing by. "Does my baby have Down syndrome?"

It was a different nurse, but she was also guarded and chose her words carefully.

"I don't know. But I can try to find someone to answer that for you. Would you like to hold your baby?"

The nurse expertly maneuvered the numerous tubes and wires attached to Fern as she placed her in my arms. Then she gave me an update. Fern was breathing on her own just fine. She was jaundice, but she did not require light therapy for the moment. She was doing a good job moderating her own body temperature with the help of just the warming table and did not require additional warming blankets under her. It appeared that, other than being small, she was perfectly healthy.

I offered Fern my breast again. I knew from reading up on birthing twins that premies don't always latch easily, so I was prepared to be patient. Never mind that Sylvan, a full two pounds heavier but only two minutes older than Fern happened to be nursing like a champ. Fern and I had a little more success nursing this time, and Theresa and I cheered!

Back in the room, Will opened the foldaway couch. Theresa, who had slept protectively at my feet as I labored through the night with Cypress, made a pallet in the corner of my hospital room. They were both soon asleep.

But sleep eluded me. A pair of air boots had been fitted to my calves to prevent blood clots from forming. Tucked somewhere near my headboard was their compressor, which made a whirring noise each time it turned on. As they inflated, the boots tightened uncomfortably around my calves. Then with a "PSHHHHHH," the compressor shut off. Over and over again, the whir startled me from the edge of sleep and as I laid there dazedly enduring the torture on my calves, a sudden "psssh" would make me flinch.

Even without the disruptive compressor and calf-crushing boots, it would have been impossible to sleep. My body hurt. The site of the cesarean incision was sore, both in a generalized way and in very specific places where stitches bit at my skin. My abdomen felt like a hollow, flabby casing holding together a pile of tender shards. Just that morning I had complained that my organs were being crowded out by the babies. Now, after being jostled and bruised by the surgeons, my battered organs had too much room to move. While they were in there, the surgeons had cut and soldered that tenuous link between my ovaries and my uterus. On top of the internal discomfort, I was still recovering from a bout of pneumonia which had landed me in the hospital only one week prior. Every time I coughed, I doubled to stabilize my tender midsection, only to immediately arch in response to the searing bolt of lightning that ripped across my lower back ribs. Everyone kept saying I was in so much pain because I'd just given birth to twins via cesarean. Later an x-ray would confirm that I had cracked rib from the wracking cough.

All the physical discomfort might have been managed with the right combination of pain medications and cough suppressants. But nothing could stop the calamity unfolding in my mind. Throughout the sleepless night, I thought on all the times my prenatal team of doctors assured me, "We are not concerned about either of your twins having Down syndrome.

They are both perfect." And yet, I was sure there was something distinctly imperfect about my daughter.

I had two babies. One, the control group, slept soundly beside me and had the wrinkly look of a newborn and also the glow of health; and one, the variant, was in the NICU thrusting her tongue, being tiny and looking very strange. Instead of answering my questions directly, the NICU night-shift nurses and resident doctors offered up plausible explanations for why my newborn daughter, Fern, was so odd-looking.

"She's a twin, so she's tiny," they said. "Her color is a little off from the jaundice. She'll pink up."

By 3 A.M., I decided I could walk myself to the NICU. I made the executive decision to remove the air boots. Quietly, I pushed Sylvan's bassinet to the side and slid out of my bed without disturbing Will and Theresa. Dragging my body hunched and sore the short distance to the NICU, I wheeled my IV bag through the double doors and discovered that Fern had been moved.

A nurse I had not seen before was changing Fern's diaper. She explained that Fern had progressed quickly from Level 3 to Level 2, a sign that she was, indeed, in good health.

I listened politely then asked, "Do you think my baby has Down syndrome?"

She responded cautiously. "I don't know. Let me get the resident on duty for you."

This time I reached for Fern myself. I jostled the wires and tubes and made Fern and myself as comfortable as possible. We tried nursing again, with little success. I gave up, opened my gown and tucked Fern's naked body against my chest.

Skin-to-skin at last. It was our first moment alone together.

She's odd looking, but there's something very compelling about her eyes.

"Hi baby. I'm your mama."

A dark-haired, doe-eyed woman introduced herself as the resident doctor on duty. "I hear you're asking whether your daughter has Down syndrome."

"Yeah. I'm sorry. I'm just trying to understand what's happening. She's so small and it seemed like my pregnancy was going fine, but now here I am with these tiny babies a month early, and I'm just looking for some kind of explanation." I couldn't stop talking. "It seems like there must be something going on if she's so tiny. And doesn't she look kind of weird to you? Plus she's not latching. And her tongue is different. What do you think? Have you ever seen a baby with Down syndrome? Do you think she has Down syndrome?"

Ms. Doe-Eyed Resident said, "I can't answer that question right now, but there are some tests we can run in the morning if you would like us to."

"Um, okay." I said.

She turned to leave. "By the way, I hear that Fern is a twin. I'm a twin too!"

I hate her. Of course she was a twin. She looked exactly like the baby girl I'd been dreaming of. Dark hair, doe-eyed and smart. Her twin was probably also good looking and doing something magnificent with his life, like being a doctor. Frankly, I didn't give a damn. Everything on my sleep-deprived body hurt, and I was starting to wonder if I was hormonally insane because of the way the nurses and doctors were walking on eggshells around me. I suspected something was wrong with my little girl, but now I wondered if this had all been just a pathetic attempt to explain to myself why I had failed to do a good job growing these babies. Whatever the case, I was not up for chitchat.

"Oh, that's nice." I said.

As I was getting ready to go back to my room, Fern's nurse approached and looked me in the eye. "You know, I've heard you asking questions all night, and I see that you are not getting a straight answer. I can't answer your questions for you, but I want you to know that you will get a straight answer when Dr. Smith is finished with her rounds tomorrow morning. You can count on that."

Gratitude took the edge off my confusion. This brave woman broke protocol and handed me a tiny piece of dignity with which to cover myself. She saw me as a person and I was grateful to learn not everyone thought I was crazy.

"Okay. Thank you." I said.

Back in my room, I nursed and changed Sylvan, leaving the diaper on the table so the night nurse could weigh it. Then I lay in my bed until day break, shifting from one uncomfortable position to another. I pressed my face to my pillow to stifle my coughs so as not to wake up Theresa and Will, and silently cursed the compressor, which still hissed and psssh-ed even though the offending calf crushers lay askew on the floor.

About an hour after sunrise, Will woke up and noticed I was staring at the ceiling. Without stirring from his nest on the couch, he asked, "How did you sleep?"

"Do you want me to say "fine" or do you want me to tell the truth?"

"I'm listening."

"I didn't sleep at all. I think there's something wrong with Fern. I don't know what it is, and they won't tell me. But they are acting weird and I'm worried."

Will had not even sat up yet. "Okay. What can I do to help?"

Has there ever been a better husband?

"Well, they said Dr. Smith would come see us after her rounds. So I guess nothing. I should call my mom."

Will handed me his cell phone, and I dialed.

"Hi Mom." This was the first time we'd chatted since I had been admitted to the hospital. Will had kept her posted on the delivery via text messaging.

"Hi! So, everything going okay?"

"Well, I'm fine. And Sylvan is beautiful and nursing like a champ. But Fern is still in the NICU. I think there's something wrong with her. I don't know what it is and I'm not going to tell you what I suspect because I don't want you to worry, but I think there's something they're not telling me. The doctor is supposed to come see us after doing rounds. I'll call you and let you know if we find out anything. For now, don't worry."

My mom was worried, of course. "Is she okay? I mean, is she breathing okay and all?"

"Yeah, mom. She's tiny. I mean, you never saw such a tiny baby. But she's fine. Look, I'll call you later. Love you."

A couple of hours later, Dr. Smith had come and gone. And my suspicion was confirmed. So it was time to call my mom with the news. I was shaking as I dialed the number.

"Hello?"

"Hi Mom. It's me."

"Oh hey! Did the doctor come see you?"

"Yeah. I have some news. Are you in a place where I can tell you something kind of bad?"

"Okay, hang on. Let me go outside." I could hear some shuffling as she left her desk and headed outside. "Okay, go ahead."

I started sobbing again, not wanting to say the words. I didn't want them to be true and if I said the words then it was going to be true. I tried to catch my breath. "Mom, Fern has Down syndrome."

My mom makes this funny little ticking noise with her mouth sometimes before she speaks when something has surprised her. She made that noise now. "Tsk! Is that all? Oh, she's going to be fine. Her grandma loves her just the same and she is going to be fine. You'll see. It's going to be fine, Heather."

I nodded and cried, unable to speak. But I was no longer sobbing, just crying. Somehow, even though I had not yet told anyone about my biggest fear, my mom had already put it to rest. Despite the fact that my daughter had Down syndrome, people were still going to love her. She was different, but she was loved. And, whether I felt like I deserved it or not, so was I.

TWO

Imperfect Love

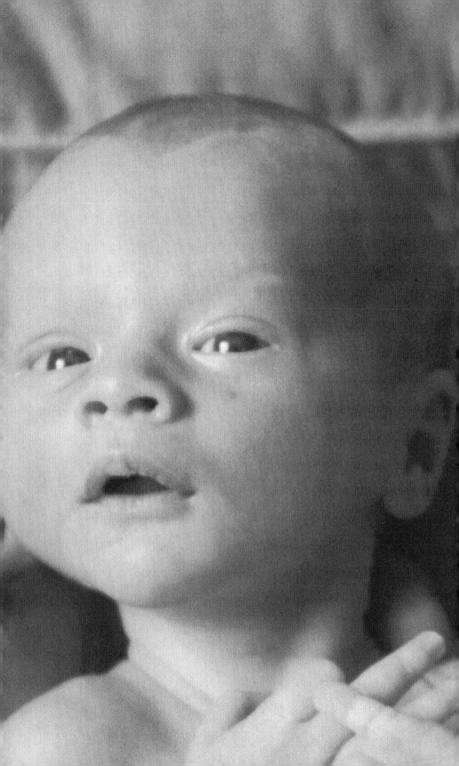

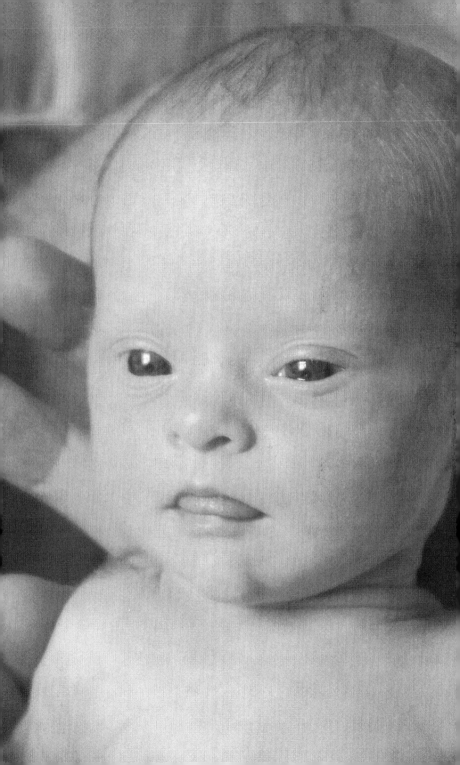

After the doctors left me to process the shocking news of Fern's diagnosis, I ranted and sobbed in protest of the unexpected arc of my life. Eventually, though, it was time to nurse.

I held an almost superstitious belief that if my babies nursed from my breasts while I was distraught, they would drink my sadness and it would affect their dispositions for life. I had to get my act together. I decided to take a shower, cesarean incision be damned.

As the water streamed over my head, I prepared myself to see Fern for the first time since receiving her diagnosis. I recalled a radio program about a well-known quadriplegic man in which he told the story of his mother's reaction when he was first handed to her. Apparently, the doctor was very cautious, saying something like, "I'm so sorry. Your baby doesn't have any arms or legs." But his mother took her baby into her arms and said, "Oh, isn't he perfect!" And that mother's belief that her baby with no arms and no legs was perfect and lovable is what made that baby grow into the strong and confident man I had heard on the radio that day.

For Fern's sake, I wanted to be that mom. I wanted to think my baby girl was perfect. I wanted to have that mom's cheery disposition and a can-do attitude, to be strong enough to love Fern unconditionally. I wanted to stride confidently through the NICU to where Fern lay in an incubator and say with a big smile, "Isn't she perfect?"

But I was not that mother.

Instead, I was the puffy-eyed mother with damp, unruly hair who dragged her wrecked body through the NICU and approached the incubator cautiously, reluctantly. I sat down in the recliner provided for parents and waited while the nurse rearranged the tangle of wires and tubes attached to Fern. Then she handed Fern down to my waiting arms.

I blinked back my tears of disappointment, forced a smile and said, "Hey there, Baby. How's it going?"

Then I began to inventory all the things that were imperfect about my daughter. She thrust her tongue. Her almond-shaped eyes looked startled. Her skin was mottled and yellow-green in color, and her arms and legs splayed in all directions.

Geez. She looks like a critter from Star Trek.

Far from perfect and lovable, I found Fern to be weird and unknowable.

I told her in a quavering voice, "Well, you aren't what I was expecting, but it's all going to work out fine. Mommy just needs to get used to her new reality." I tried and failed to nurse Fern, then placed her back in her incubator where I changed her impossibly tiny diaper.

As I raised the railing and prepared to leave, Fern's nurse approached and said, "Looks like you're an old pro." She knew that I now knew, and there was nothing to do but force another smile and return to my room.

I put myself on a three-hour rotation, and spent the first ninety minutes with Sylvan, who should have been easy to love. He was beautiful, fine-boned and pink. He nursed heartily and slept contentedly. He had amazing deep blue eyes and the cutest pointy chin I'd ever laid eyes on. But I was too distracted by the implications of Fern's diagnosis to properly love him either, too confused by the feelings of guilt already plaguing me. How could I love Sylvan if I could barely stand to look at Fern? Was it okay to still nurse Sylvan when it was so difficult for Fern to latch? Shouldn't I spend every possible minute with Fern, because she was the one in the NICU? Or maybe I should spend more time with Sylvan, because it wasn't fair to ask him to live in the shadow of Fern's diagnosis from day one.

I knew that being the mother of twins was going to be hard, but this unexpected turn of events created an emotional landmine. Holding Sylvan against my chest, the weight of him so much more substantial and taunt than Fern's floppy, hypotonic body, I found myself withholding kisses to his downy head out of fairness to Fern. The guilt I felt for essentially rejecting Fern on some level was compounded by the guilt I felt for being drawn to Sylvan.

It would be weeks before I realized that withholding love from one person does not create more love for another.

When Sylvan's time was up, I spent the next ninety minutes with Fern in the NICU. Right from the start, I realized I couldn't fool Fern. Even at only a few hours old, Fern locked eyes with mine and commanded I take notice of the intelligence in them. Intelligence I was not expecting to find.

She sees me. She is discerning. She knows who I am among all these nurses.

Although I was having difficulty stepping into the romanticized role of Loving Mother, Fern seemed to easily accept that I was her mother and trusted that I was the one who would care for her. Despite the dozens of people handling her every day, she had imprinted on me, like a baby duck. Fern's responsiveness to me triggered an instinctive desire to do everything necessary to protect and nurture her.

During her stay in the NICU, I worked with every lactation consultant on site to help Fern learn to nurse, insisting she not be offered a pacifier or a bottle. When it became apparent Fern would not be able to latch to nurse, I insisted on being the one to feed her around the clock, first with a syringe and then with a bottle. I changed her diapers, chose her tiny preemie outfits and consulted with the doctors about every aspect of her care. I just kept showing up, giving her what I had to give. It was a kind of "fake it until you make it" approach.

In return, Fern perked up when she heard my voice as I approached her incubator. She allowed me to comfort her when the nurses pricked her heels over and over again to draw blood. She looked at me in wonder when I sang, and she held my finger as she dozed on my chest. We were warm together in that chilly hospital, getting to know each other through the osmosis of our shared heat.

Resting with Fern on my chest, I thought about the interview with the quadriplegic. The way he told the story of his mother, recalled it in such vivid detail, it was as if he was actually there. Of course he *was* there, but he was just a newborn and he could not have possibly understood what was going on.

Or did he?

There was never any question that I wanted to be Fern's mother. I just didn't want her to have Down syndrome and, for reasons I am still sorting out, I lacked whatever was required of a person to feel instant love for a child who has special needs. So while I lived in a confused place of wanting, but not really loving, Fern, I promised to never let her see me mourn her diagnosis, lest she think I was mourning her existence.

If Fern does have any recollection of those early days, her memories won't be of a mother gushing with wonder and exclaiming, "She's perfect!" But I'm pretty sure she will understand my intention, the effort that stood in the place of love. The unexpected situation demanded maturity and resolve, a kind of strength I was surprised to find I had. We may not have had the dreamlike mother-and-child bond you see in tear-jerking commercials, but our now powerful and consuming love is made from the same stuff that holds together marriages and forms the bedrock of friendships that last a lifetime. The mortar between this uncertain mother and her vulnerable baby was simply the will to try.

THREE

Congratulations

I stopped mid-chew. "Oh my god."

My husband looked up from his chili. "What?"

I set my fork down and swallowed my bite. "Oh. My. God. I know who it's from."

My husband was confused. "What? Who?"

Tears welled up in my eyes and I had to look at the ceiling to keep from crying. "The gift by Fern's bed. It's from Lucey."

Will propped his elbows on the hospital café table and looked at me for more.

I was smiling and shaking my head, trying to breathe back the tears. "The gift! It's from Lucey, who has Lili."

"Okay?"

"Down syndrome Lili!"

Suddenly, he understood. I had to put my head down on the café table to cry and laugh over the irony.

The gift was the kind of thing you would expect for a newborn baby girl. Cute, pretty, small. It was in an innocuous gift bag, and inside there was a card signed, "Lucey, John and Lili." For hours, it had nagged at me. Who could have possibly gotten a gift to Fern's crib side in the NICU?

Naturally, my first thought was that it was from Midwife Lucy. But she was Lucy without an "e" and she had always called or texted before she made the long drive to the hospital. Besides, she would have just handed us the gift, as she had been doing all week. She was as practical as she was generous, never coy. Not surprisingly, when we texted her about the gift, she knew nothing about it.

Our friends Jill and Theresa were on the "family" list, which meant they could come and go in the NICU as they pleased, but neither of them knew anything about the gift.

It was a mystery. With little to go on, and tons to do, the day progressed, following the strange rhythm that emerges when you're caring for a loved one in the hospital. Meet with doctors. Hold your loved one's hand. Wait for test results. Sleep when you can. Occasionally get something to eat.

Lucey, John and Lili? Did I know these people? Was this gift actually meant for Fern? I asked Fern's attending nurse if she saw who brought the gift. She didn't know anything about it. "It was here when I started my shift," she said.

We were left to puzzle it out, which is what we were doing in the hospital café when it hit me: it was Lucey, mother of Lili, who had Down syndrome. Why, she must have driven almost 90 minutes each way to deliver a gift to Fern's crib side.

I had met Lucey almost four years prior when she worked in the office next door to mine. Every now and then she had her very adorable, extremely well-dressed little girl in tow. Even to my untrained eye, it was clear the child, Lili, had Down syndrome. Our offices shared a kitchen and one day when Lucey and I were making our lunches, I screwed up my courage to ask Lucey something that had been weighing on me.

I said, "Do you mind if I ask you a personal question?"

"Sure," she said.

"Lili has Down syndrome, right?"

"She sure does."

"Well, I'm 37 and I'm thinking of getting pregnant. Given the increased odds that I could have a child who has Down syndrome, I'm just wondering if you might tell me what it's like."

Lucey gave me a big smile and said, "It's like being invited into a world I never knew existed and I'm so glad I'm here." Lucey said a lot more that day, but that part stuck with me. It was like an invitation. One that she was glad to have received.

I got pregnant the next month and went on to have Cypress, a healthy "normal" child. And because I quit my job to stay home with Cypress, I didn't see Lucey again for a couple of years. In fact, it wasn't until I was very pregnant with the twins that I ran into Lucey. As it turned out, she was the next-door neighbor of one of my friends, who also had a little boy Cypress's age. Lucey's visiting nephew was the same age as Cypress and my friend's son, so we had an impromptu play date for the three boys. Lili was at school, so Lucey and I passed a lovely couple of hours on a warm day with three small boys playing on the swing set together. After I left to take the boys home for a nap, I never contacted Lucey again. We weren't even friends on Facebook. Kindred, but busy, spirits.

Until Fern was born. Until this gift. Lucey had heard from her neighbor that my little girl had been born with Down syndrome. I guess Lucey wanted to be one of the first people to welcome me and Fern into this new world, to remind me that one day I might also be happy to have received an exclusive invite.

I have often wondered what it would have been like had we seen Lucey that day, if we hadn't been tending to some other piece of hospital business when she made her way to the NICU to leave a gift at the front desk. It didn't matter. She included a card with exactly the message we needed to hear from the only person I'd ever met who could possibly understand.

It read: "Congratulations on your new baby! Love, Lucey, John and Lili."

FOUR

Married to the Modern Medical Machine

I don't like dealing with the Modern Medicine Machine. It seems to me that there is a certain kind of learned helplessness emerging and, simultaneously, a crisis of health. Instead of taking charge of their diet or lifestyle, some people seem happier bringing their broken health problems to a doctor to fix.

It would be easy to blame Fern's diagnosis for why we suddenly felt married to the Modern Medical Machine. Before Fern was born, Will and I rarely went to the doctor. Then Cypress was born at home, and when it came to caring for Cypress, we relied on home remedies and staggered his vaccines. In stark contrast, after Fern was born, we visited or were visited by at least one doctor every few days for weeks on end.

But looking back, I see that we first became engaged, and even beholden, to the Modern Medical Machine from the moment we found out we were having twins. When the nurse conducting the transvaginal confirmation ultrasound announced, "You're going to have TWO babies!" the tears I cried were not, I'm a little ashamed to say, tears of joy. In addition to being twice as scared about having twice as many opportunities to screw up twice as many children, I was also mourning the lost opportunity to have another amazing homebirth experience.

Growing up, we had a house, food, clothes and transportation, but there wasn't a whole lot more on top of that. While my friends snacked on name-brand Pop Tarts™ and played their *Ataris*, we ate peanut butter and jelly sandwiches on bread from the day-old shop and were told to play outside until dinner time. If it weren't for my father's disgust for government handouts, we would have been perfect candidates for food and medical assistance. Instead, my mother was thrifty. Even on her meager pay, my mother pulled together a healthy, balanced dinner and we sat down as a family to eat together every night.

And whether it was because we did not have good health insurance or my mom could not afford the time off to take us, we rarely went to the doctor. Unless you were hemorrhaging or suffocating, my mom had the confidence to try a home remedy before rushing to see a doctor. As a kid, I smirked when my friends went to the doctor for something as common as pink eye or a sprained ankle. My mom kept a stash of boric acid for ailments of the eye, and the best you could hope for was ice and an ace bandage for the ankle. These were the kind of things we were expected to push through. And we did.

If my belief that going to the doctor was a sign of weakness, it was born from the hubris of a poor kid who needed to turn the thing that made them different from everyone else into something that made them better than everyone else. And it was the experience of living in Penns Valley that nurtured that belief into conviction. The area is notable for its beautiful rolling hills (like the Berkshires but without the attitude or fancy SUV's), and is populated by an interesting mix of college professors, blue-collar locals, Amish and back-to-the-landers. Experienced midwives are an everyday part of our community, so stories of beautiful, peaceful homebirths weave their way into everyday conversation. By the time I got pregnant with my first child, I'd heard dozens of homebirth stories and considered homebirth not only a viable option, but the superior choice.

But our insurance would not cover a homebirth. It was going to cost us several thousand dollars out of pocket to have a homebirth, so we carefully weighed the possibility of having our first born child in a hospital.

In the end, it really just came down to attitudes. During a routine prenatal exam with a member of the hospital team, I said, "Dr. Qaaid, you are a man from Africa. You have seen women labor naturally and you know that they can give birth without the use of epidurals, even if the labors are long. Surely you support my desire to have a natural birth?"

He gave me a good natured smile. "Yes, it can be done. But you are a woman in America and it is because I've seen natural labor that I do not understand why you would ever refuse an epidural."

In a similar conversation with Midwife Lucy, I said, "I feel like I might actually be looking forward to labor,"

She answered, "Of course you are! You're going to do great."

I didn't have any serious reservations about the obstetrics team at the local hospital. They had the reputation for being pushy and distant, but I knew they would do an adequate job of delivering my baby and caring for my health. Instead, it was Midwife Lucy's warmth and professionalism that was a more powerful draw. Lucy had years of experience with an impeccable track record and, more importantly, an unshakable faith in a woman's body to birth naturally. When Midwife Lucy was able to provide a back-up doctor who had admitting rights to a hospital in a nearby town, our minds were made up. We would welcome our first born son into our home, at home.

Had we gone with the Modern Medical Machine for Cypress's birth, I would have surely had a c-section. The labor was almost 40 hours long and I pushed for six hours. A conventional doctor would likely have started saying things like, "The labor has stalled. Let's try petocin," and, "The baby is stuck. I recommend a C-section." But Midwife Lucy had seen longer and harder labors, and she had unshakeable confidence in my body's ability to birth my child. She and her assistant constantly monitored the baby, whose steady and strong heartbeat never faltered, not even once, through the entirety of the labor. We had been meeting with Midwife Lucy for months, and we had appreciated her professionalism and knowledge. But it wasn't until we saw her focused, single-minded attention to duty, that of caring for me and my unborn child, that we really understood what a gifted and talented midwife she was. And it took months for us to fully appreciate what an amazing gift she had given us.

As much as I wanted to replicate the amazing, life-transforming experience of birthing a child at home, I never seriously considered birthing the twins anywhere other than a hospital. Sure, I had fantasies that Will and I would be enjoying a Sunday drive through the woods when I went into labor. Will would pull over to the side of the road and the twins would come quickly and painlessly. I would be lauded for years to come as the amazing woman who gave birth to twins effortlessly and with grace. In the woods! But that was all just fantasy.

Resigned to working with conventional care providers within the Modern Medical Machine, I asked Lucy if she would still be our midwife, my line to sanity, a voice of reason who "got" that what I wanted from a pregnancy and delivery wasn't silly. We came up with a great system for working with the doctors and midwives at Lutheran Community Hospital. In the beginning, the midwives were just monitoring my pee and blood pressure. They agreed I could do every other visit with Midwife Lucy, who would send them the updates to be kept in my medical records. This saved me two hours of driving and also allowed me to spend time in Midwife Lucy's relaxed and capable company. We might curl up on her daybed and read the latest statistics I'd come across, or spend the hour with her patiently listening to me reason out how everything was going to be fine if I could only gain more weight. The other half of the time, I traveled to Lutheran.

The Modern Medical Machine was intimidating and confusing. Looking back, I asked all the wrong questions. I was so focused on what I wanted (to work with a team that supported my desire to deliver my twins vaginally), I didn't see what I needed (a medical team of highly qualified, experienced professionals). The thing about doctors is that I can never figure out who to trust. They all seem so confident in themselves. I can't tell who is a good doctor and who is a bad doctor. And, it turns out, there are plenty of bad doctors.

FIVE

Clues

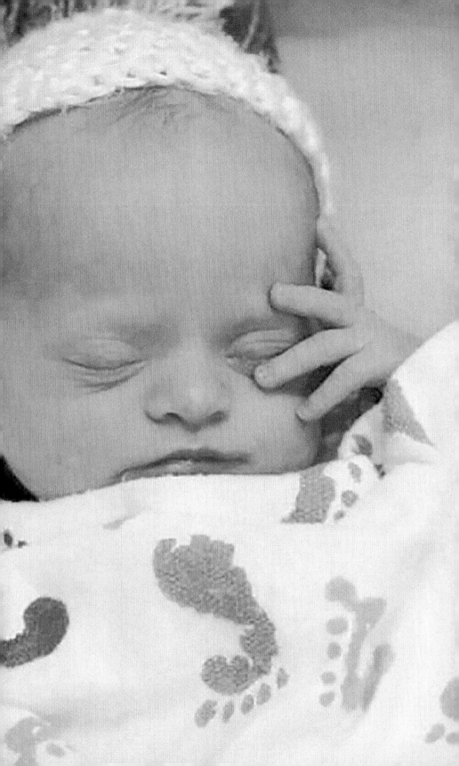

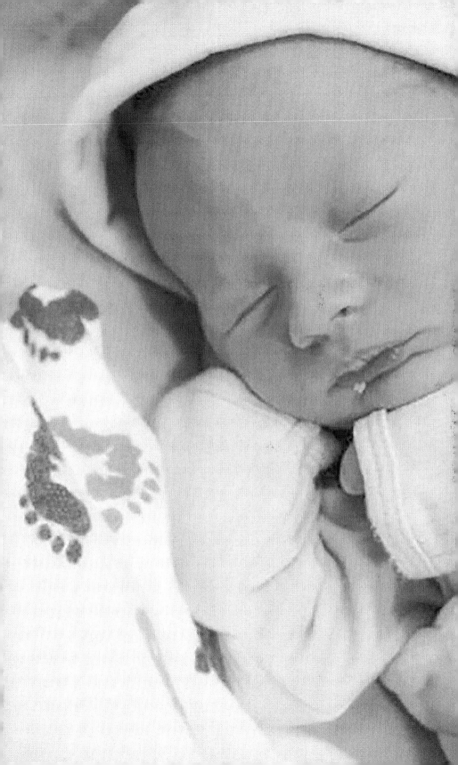

You'd think from all the cursing and crying I did upon learning that Fern had Down syndrome that her diagnosis came out of the blue. In reality, it wasn't a complete surprise. There were, after all, the prenatal test results.

From the minute I pushed PLAY on the answering machine and heard all the unsaid words between "Hello. This is Dr. Odongo," and "Please return my call as soon as possible," I knew we were in for some bad news. And I was sure it had to do with the results of the Quad Screening for the twins.

I waited until Will could be home to return Dr. Odongo's call. A light snow was falling outside when we put Cypress down for a nap and crawled on top of our comforter to huddle around the phone. Nervous, I punched in the telephone number and adjusted the volume on speakerphone.

The nurse who answered the phone seemed to know who I was. "Yes, Ms. House. Hold on a second while I go find Dr. Odongo."

My sense of uneasiness grew stronger.

Why is she going to get the doctor in the middle of a busy day? Why can't she just relay the message to me?

After a few minutes of holding, the nurse picked up the line again. "Ms. House? Can you just hold a little longer? We're trying to find the file for Dr. Odongo."

"Sure," I said lightly even though the butterflies in my stomach had turned into ravens, beating their wings against my ribs and pecking at my throat to get out.

I started calculating my options. At just 15-weeks pregnant, I could still have an abortion if there was something horrifically wrong. I wondered whether I could have a selective reduction (euphemism for aborting just one of multiple babies) if one child was okay but the other wasn't.

I looked at Will, wondering what was going through his mind. He gave me a little smile.

"Hello?" Dr. Odongo said. She sounded a little breathless. "Thank you for waiting."

This was the first time we had ever spoken to Dr. Odongo. So far we had only met with the hospital's nurse practitioner midwives.

"Okay, I can't find the file," she said with a thick African accent. "But I think I can remember the gist of things. Basically, the screening has come back and there is an increased chance that both of your babies have Down syndrome," she said. "We can't be 100% sure, but I'd like to do some follow up tests."

Both of the babies? If Will was as stunned as I was, he didn't let on. As I reached to pick up the phone, Will laid back on a pillow.

I held the phone so I could speak directly into the mic. "What kind of probability are we talking here?"

I need numbers.

"Well, I can't remember the precise numbers right now, just that the risk was significantly elevated," Dr. Odongo replied.

I persisted. "Can you even give me a ballpark? Like…are we talking a 1 in 10 chance?"

"Oh, no. Not that strong. Ah! Here! Here is the file. Let's see…"

I looked at Will with raised eyebrows and shook my head, and he knew what I was thinking. *Can you believe this?* I could hear her flipping through pages.

"Okay," she said, "For Baby A, the risk is 1 in 252 and for Baby B…" more flipping of pages, "it is also 1 in 252."

"I see." I said, instantly recalling that the results of Cypress's screening estimated the risk of him being born with Down syndrome to be a scant 1 in 6000. Still. I was encouraged. There was a 251 chance in 252 that the babies would be just fine.

"So, if my math is right, there is less than a 1% chance that the kids have Down syndrome, right?"

Just fifteen weeks into this pregnancy and I was already feeling taxed by how the Modern Medical Machine is designed to expose a problem where there may not be one.

Dr. Odongo maintained her position. "I can't really say that. All I can say is that the risk is elevated."

I practically rolled my eyes. "But if the risk is 1 in 252, then there is a very strong possibility that neither of the kids have Down syndrome. Right? It is math," I said, exasperated with "protocol" and unnecessary tests littered with false positives and skewed results.

"Well," Dr. Odongo answered cautiously, "It doesn't exactly work that way. For your age, the acceptable level of risk is 1 in 270. At 1 in 252, the risk is elevated."

To me, this did not sound like much elevation. "Yes, 1 in 252 is more probable than 1 in 270, but still," I said cautiously as it began to dawn on me that I was arguing about something I did not quite understand with someone who was an expert on the matter. My voice went up an octave. "It's not 1 in 10, right?"

I looked at Will again. *Why do I have to do all the work to make myself feel better?*

Dr. O cleared her throat. "My recommendation is that you have a follow up ultrasound with MFM and perhaps an amniocentesis."

"MFM?" I asked.

"Maternal Fetal Medicine," Dr. Odongo explained. "We consider this a high risk pregnancy and MFM can give us a better idea of how the babies are doing."

There was that phrase again: high risk. But was the doctor saying that my pregnancy was high-risk because of my age, or because of the results of the Quad Screening? Either way, I didn't like the implication of either me or my children being treated as "high risk." Risk is something to be avoided or, at the very least, managed, and I didn't like the idea of being managed, or my children being avoided.

Meanwhile, the words "Elderly Multigravida" were on my permanent record. It refers to the second (or more) pregnancy in a woman who will be 35 years of age or older at expected date of delivery, and conventional practitioners classify these pregnancies as "high risk."

I bucked against the label every time someone tried to stick it on me. I recognized that, technically, I fit the definition. At 39-years-old, I was almost always the oldest expectant mother in the waiting area at the doctor's office. And I was expecting twins, so I understood that it *looked* like a high risk pregnancy on paper. But it didn't *feel* like a high risk pregnancy to me. The other women in the lobby might have been half my age, but many of them were obese, or smelled of stale smoke. They hadn't traveled, or finished advanced degrees or delivered a baby on their living room floor. I was fit. I was healthy. My blood pressure was a respectable 108 over 60, and I didn't have any swelling. For Pete's sake, I didn't even have stretch marks! To me it seemed obvious that I wasn't your average woman of "advanced maternal age."

Months later, after the twins were delivered via C-section and Fern did, in fact, have Down syndrome, and I had to concede the correlation between her diagnosis and my choice to have children later in life, and there was still discord between how I perceived myself (as a young, lithesome woman barely 20-years-old) and reality (a middle-aged mother of three who had just delivered a child with special needs). Nothing illustrates this as well as the time when I was throwing myself a pity party about Fern having Down syndrome. I complained to my mother, "Fern will probably still live with me when I'm 50!" To which my mother responded, "Well, yeah Heather. You're 40. She'll only be ten years old."

To me, Maternal Fetal Medicine was for women who were having problem pregnancies, and in my pre-Fern haughty and overly-high-opinion-of-oneself days, I didn't think we had a problem. I told Dr. Odongo, "Whether one or both of our kids has Down syndrome, we're keeping the babies. And we won't *risk* a miscarriage with an amnio. So," I asked, "Is there any point in having the higher level ultrasound with MFM?"

Dr. Odongo answered. "Well, there are some health issues that are more prevalent in children with Down syndrome, so the outcomes for those babies are better if we can identify the issues before birth."

That babies who were born with Down syndrome could have health issues was news to me. I just thought they were slow and kind of strange-looking. I reluctantly agreed to the higher level ultrasound with Maternal Fetal Medicine.

Within a few minutes of hanging up with Dr. Odongo, I Googled nothing about Down syndrome but everything that brought into question the reliability of the Quad Screening. The test, which looks for four specific substances in the mother's blood to determine if there is an increased or decreased probability of the baby being born with a birth defect, is generally recommended for pregnant women over the age of 35. The Quad Screening predicts the likelihood of a problem; it does not provide a definitive diagnosis. And the Quad is notoriously unreliable. High detection rates are common in the case of older women, and especially common in the case of twins. I was certain we were dealing with false positives and everything would turn out to be fine.

We scheduled the ultrasound with Maternal Fetal Medicine for the following Thursday, and Will took the day off work to drive me to the hospital. The office of the OB/GYN Associates was in the old wing of Lutheran Community Hospital. Forsaking our local hospital, I chose Lutheran, which was located over an hour from our home, precisely because it was *not* the most advanced modern medical facility. Lutheran still employed certified nurse midwives who worked with a large population of Mennonites and Amish in the area. It was my hope that I would be able to do my prenatal care and delivery with these midwives, women who still believed giving birth was a natural event, not a medical emergency.

Will dropped me at the entrance of an outdated building. Looking back, I remember the dread I felt upon entering the drab building and I wonder if that was because I knew in my heart of hearts, this wasn't the right place for my prenatal care. I made my way through the dark corridors to the windowless office of OB/GYN. As would be the case throughout my pregnancy, the office was running late and it was another 30 minutes of entertaining a 14-month-old in the lobby before I was called back to the small room containing the ultrasound machine.

The room was a typical exam room with one notable exception: instead of the bright overhead fluorescent lights, the room was lit with a single, mellow lamp which cast a yellow glow. The effect, if not exactly homey, was at least a welcome contrast to the glaring light of the halls. The Maternal Fetal Medicine technician asked me to remove my pants and underwear, lay on the table and cover my lower half with the paper sheet.

The higher order ultrasound is used to measure specific parts of the baby's body in utero to determine whether a baby is likely to have any "defects," a term with which I now take exception. Our plan was to get through this ultrasound and hopefully not need to be in touch with MFM again. Will did his best to keep Cypress occupied in the small room as I laid on my back for 75 minutes while the ultrasound tech measured every little bit of each of my babies. She began with Baby A.

"Do you want to know the gender of the babies?" she asked.

Will answered, "Not really," but the technician couldn't hear him over my enthusiastic "Absolutely!"

I was hoping for a boy/girl set. In my mind, this would be the perfect combination for our family. Cypress could have a little brother to play with, and the twins would have their own special thing. Two girls was, well, unthinkable. As was having a total of three boys!

She started with Baby A. "It's a boy."

Then she was silent for a long time as she punched keys and made slight movements with the wand. I was desperate to know the gender of Baby B, but the tech was systematic and I respected her concentration. Every now and then I made out a body part. "That's a profile of the face!" I said, and the tech nodded and pointed to an arm to orient me to the position of the baby.

After 45 minutes, it was time to measure Baby B.

I suddenly saw three tell-tale white lines indicating a vagina and piped excitedly, "It's a girl!"

"Yes, it's a girl" the tech confirmed, as tears streamed down my face. It's the only time I remember being truly happy during my pregnancy with the twins. I knew we would call her Fern.

When everyone was measured and accounted for, the tech wiped the goo off my belly and brought me slowly to an upright position. I got dressed and shared a snack with Cypress to stave off our hungries while we waited for the doctor.

Dr. Menendez was a good looking man with a tidy salt and pepper crew cut. He introduced himself by shaking my hand, then Will's, then Cypress's. Then he opened the chart.

"It looks like Baby A is just fine, but Baby B's kidney is measuring slightly dilated," he said.

"So do you think she has Down syndrome?" I asked.

Dr. Menendez said, "Well, I cannot say for sure, but it seems unlikely. The kidney is a soft marker. All the hard markers, like the size of the femur and the thickness of the back of her neck, are measuring normal. But we'll keep an eye on the kidney to be sure." Dr. Menendez referenced the chart quickly and looked back up to say, "I'd like to see you in two weeks."

Wait. I thought this was a once and done.

"But I don't want to come back if I don't need to. I'd prefer to stick with the midwives. I only agreed to this ultrasound to see if the babies have Down syndrome," I said.

Dr. Menendez seemed perplexed and I realized that he was hearing this information for the first time. He did not know that I was trying to avoid having a relationship with Maternal Fetal Medicine. He did not know that my goal was to keep this pregnancy as simple as possible. As understanding dawned on him, I imagined Dr. Menendez was thinking, "Lady, what part of 'high risk pregnancy' don't you understand?" Advocating for myself within the Modern Medical Machine was already starting to feel like a lot of hard work. By wanting to do something different from the usual plan, I inadvertently threw the doctors a curve ball and, in turn, their confusion flustered me.

Instead he said, "I see. Well, I'd still like to see you in two weeks to keep an eye on Baby B's kidney. If it doesn't resolve itself, we may want to take special precautions at birth."

Two weeks later, Cypress and I made the hour drive by ourselves and I laid uncomfortably on my back for another 75-minute ultrasound, while Cypress busied himself with the puzzles and snacks I had brought for him. When the tech was finished measuring I asked her if the kidney of Baby B had changed.

"What?" she asked, confused.

I reminded her that I was back because we were keeping an eye on the kidney because it was a soft marker for Down syndrome and it was slightly dilated two weeks prior. She opened the file and nodded in agreement. "Yeah, it was. Well, I'd better get that measurement."

I was annoyed. *Are you, or are you not, keeping an eye on the kidney? Why do I have to remind you of why I am here?*

This time, a different doctor came in to debrief with me. I do not remember him introducing himself.

"Everything looks good," he said, without looking up from the file to greet me or Cypress.

I bent to catch his eye. "So you don't think she has Down syndrome?"

"What?" He flipped casually through my chart.

I couldn't help letting my annoyance show. "We are here because the blood work showed an elevated risk of Down syndrome. And two weeks ago Dr. Menendez said Baby B's kidney was slightly dilated, which he said was a soft marker but that it was worth keeping an eye on."

"No, no," the nameless doctor said, brushing my concerns aside. "We're just keeping an eye on your cervix. We're not concerned about your daughter having Down syndrome. Everything looks fine."

I very much wanted to believe this person. His words should have been comforting. But I didn't think he had so much as looked at my file before stepping into the room, and he certainly wasn't making much of an effort to listen to me. I doubted he had much of a grasp on the situation. I was learning not all doctors are created equal.

He finally looked up from the file to say, "I'd like to see you again in two weeks."

"But I thought you said everything looks fine," I said. "I don't see the need for another 75-minute ultrasound."

"Well yes. Everything looks fine *so far.* But you are considered a high risk pregnancy and we want to keep a close eye on you."

I agreed to *one more* higher order ultrasound, mostly because I wanted some assurance that Baby B's kidney was the right size. So six weeks after our initial phone call with Dr. O, I laid down for a third uncomfortable 75-minute ultrasound, again with Cypress in tow.

I was relieved when Dr. Menendez, and not the other doctor, walked in. I liked Dr. Menendez. He was friendly. He acknowledged Cypress's presence. He took the time to answer all of my questions. It seemed he finally understood that I wanted to work with the midwives and only use the services of Maternal Fetal Medicine if an actual problem developed, and he did not seem to take this personally. It felt like he was on my team.

He shook my hand and gave Cypress a high-five then said, "Everything looks good."

I explained to him my confusion about whether we were actually watching Baby B for Down syndrome or not, told him about having to remind the ultrasound technician to measure the kidney during my previous visit.

"No, she's fine. Everything is measuring normal and the kidney seems to have worked itself out."

Dr. Menendez looked me in the eye when he said this. He seemed relaxed, and earnest, and thorough. I figured this must be how it worked: the Modern Medicine Machine detected a potential problem, and the Modern Medicine Machine used technology and people smarter than me to confirm there was no actual problem.

Over the next several months, as my belly grew bigger and time on my back grew unbearable, I continued my care with the nurse midwives and their ultrasound technician, Ned. Ned was a middle-aged fellow who wore nice ties and round spectacles and always greeted me with a friendly smile. As long as I agreed to return to MFM when he didn't feel he was qualified to make a decision, Ned seemed happy to provide his service for this almost-40 year-old mother-of-twins-to-be who did not consider her pregnancy to be high risk. And, per our agreement, every time the slightest problem was detected, off I went to MFM for another higher level ultrasound.

At week 33, when the growth differentiation between the babies started to approach 10%, Ned warned me that this was getting to be out of his league and that we probably wouldn't see each other again as I was squarely on Maternal Fetal Medicine turf. He also warned me that I was likely heading for a C-section given that both the babies were breech. I had long put the question of whether one of the twins had Down syndrome out of my mind, until this growth difference started to emerge. Now, despite what the doctors were saying, I was beginning to have my own doubts.

I confided to Theresa that I wondered if perhaps the reason Baby B was growing so slowly was because there was something wrong with her.

Theresa asked, "What do you think might be wrong with her that the doctors haven't found?"

"I don't know. They say she doesn't have Down syndrome. Maybe she's just retarded." Then I threw my head back and blew out my breath. "And I really do not want to be in the Mothers of Retards club!" I actually said those appalling words. Out loud.

Concerned about Baby B's lagging growth at week 34, I went once more to Maternal Fetal Medicine. This time they measured the blood flow in the umbilical cord and pressure in the hearts. They were looking for signs that the placenta was aging faster than the babies, or that intrauteral growth restriction was developing.

That day, the ultrasound tech was emailing results to the doctor who was in another town. As usual, they were running late and I was in the small lobby entertaining Cypress when the young patient before me was called into a private room to discuss the results of her ultrasound with the doctor via Skype. After about 20 minutes, the young patient came out of the room in a whirl of emotion and left the building crying. Clearly, the news was not good. So when the tech sent my results to the doctor and he had texted her right back "All looks good," I thought, *Well, it must.* I mean, he didn't even want to hold face time with me via Skype, so I assumed there was, once again, nothing interesting to report.

Predictably, the tech said, "We'd like to see you again next week." And, just as predictably, I rolled my eyes as I made the appointment.

Despite my resistance to the Modern Medical Machine, during the course of my 36-week pregnancy, I consented to their litany of tests and had 17 ultrasounds, six of which were of the higher level. And, in following their recommendations, I assumed that we had all the information we could possibly gather about the two babies I was growing in my belly. Other than Baby B growing a bit slower than Baby A, the Modern Medicine Machine promised over and over again that everything was just fine. And I believed them.

SIX

Early Labor

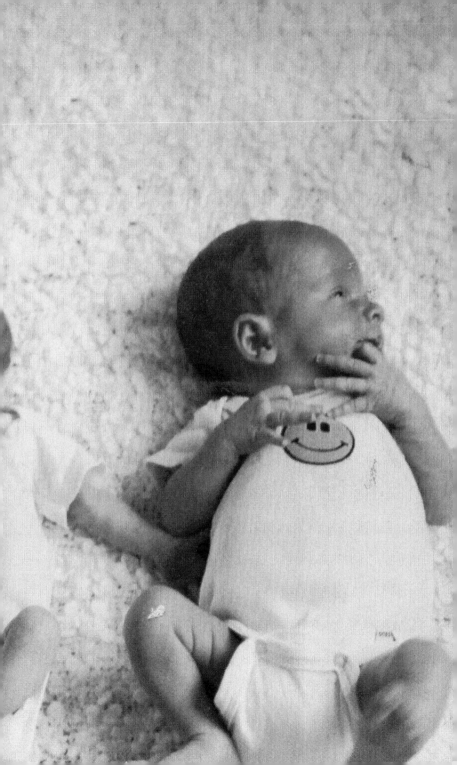

I continued my care with Lutheran, seeing the folks with Maternal Fetal Medicine as deemed necessary, checking in with Midwife Lucy in the interim. In great contrast to the depressing halls of Lutheran, Midwife Lucy and I sat next to each other on her comfy couch in her cheerful birthing center as I went through one alarming scenario after another, and she patiently doled out sage advice on how to retain control over my prenatal care.

Then I got sick. Really sick. At first, it just seemed like I had an annoying cough brought on by a combination of bad allergies and a sensitive throat. At 34 weeks pregnant with twins, my body was full of babies and there wasn't room for even a tickle in my throat. The cough worsened. Several times a day what started out as a tickle would escalate into a violent cough and I would vomit what little food I had managed to keep down. This was upsetting because I was doing everything I could to gain weight. I tried every natural remedy in the book until I finally overcame my resistance and got myself to the walk-in clinic for antibiotics. But it was too little, too late.

That evening, with antibiotics coursing through my blood and cough suppressants on my tongue, I started vomiting with feverish chills. Although going to the emergency room seemed not only logical but imperative, I was really concerned about losing what little control I had retained over my prenatal care. My prenatal care had hardly been ideal, but there was still a chance I could deliver with the midwives or at least enjoy their female company post-cesarean. I was leery about going to our local hospital, where Dr. Qaaid worked, where I didn't feel welcomed and which I'd worked so hard to avoid. I was worried the doctors would insist on keeping me overnight or, worse, try to convince me to have a C-section as soon as possible.

There was a moment of hesitation at the kitchen door where I stood and said aloud, "Do I really feel bad enough to go?" Then another wave of nausea overtook me and I stumbled out the door to the car, leaving Theresa and her husband Glenn to care for Cypress.

A few minutes later, we were cresting the mountain between our house and the hospital. Even though I was miserable and hacking and who-knows-what-shade-of-green, Will was, as always, steadfast and focused.

Suddenly, I felt a tightening in my lower abdomen. "Crap." I muttered.

"What?" asked Will.

"I just had a contraction." Defeat began to set in. This wasn't good. In fact, it was everything I DIDn't want. It was too early. Baby B was too small. I didn't have faith in the local hospital. And, more than anything, I did not want to risk having my twins delivered at one hospital, then transported to another for more intensive care while I stayed behind, separated from them until I could be discharged or transferred.

The plan is to have two healthy babies who are not tiny in a friendly hospital, so tonight really isn't a good time to be having these babies.

Breathe.

Will drove in silence while I focused on my body. Weirdly, I had gone into labor with our first child on this very stretch of road over this very mountain. Will didn't believe me when I told him I was in labor with Cypress, but he knew better than to doubt me this time. The contractions came four minutes apart, lasting just shy of one minute. The pain was not intense, but there was no denying what was happening.

I turned to Will, "Don't worry. They can stop the contractions with an injection of magnesium." I must have picked up this bit of information from one of the many books I'd read, and I presented it to Will as if it was a simple fact. He remained silent, staring at the road straight ahead.

In the hospital's circular drop-off, Will jumped out of the car and grabbed a wheelchair. I didn't want to need a wheelchair, but I felt terrible. Plus, I knew walking would only make the contractions worse.

Will wheeled me to the check-in desk.

The receptionist eyed my huge belly. "Are you here because you're in labor, or for something else?"

Tears welled up in my eyes and I choked on my words. "I don't know."

Will went to park the car, leaving me to explain how my coughing and vomiting had brought on contractions. The receptionist handed me a beeper just as Will returned, and we took our places in the lobby to wait. I sat in my wheelchair watching television, hoping the banality of late night talk shows would take my mind off of what was happening. It was a slow night and we didn't even watch a full skit before my name was called and we were escorted to triage.

There was some debate about where to send me. Although I insisted I was there because of my cough and fever, the contractions threw the triage nurse a curveball. I wasn't in active labor, but she was concerned that if active labor were to start, they would have to move me to the maternity wing. She decided to admit me to the maternity ward and have a doctor from internal medicine pay me a visit there.

They wheeled me through the labyrinth of the hospital to the maternity ward and left me in the care of a two seasoned nurses, one dressed in scrubs printed with Looney Tunes characters, the other dressed in neon pink. I tried to keep them focused on my primary reason for being there, explaining that, despite the fact that I was having contractions, I was not there because I was in labor. I really just wanted help for my cough. Once we got my cough under control, I insisted, I knew I could get the contractions under control.

The nurses looked at me dubiously. At this late hour, neither of their outfits seemed to suit their dispositions. Nurse Looney Tunes did not seem goofy or able to see the hilarity in life, and Nurse Neon Pink did not have a particular brightness about her. I could see them trying to work out whether I was in denial brought on by hormonally induced insanity.

"Really, the contractions only started because of my cough," I said, between hacking fits. "If I could stop this cough, I know that I could relax enough to make the contractions subside."

They exchanged a look as they jointly decided I might be one of those "Mind Over Body" freaks, and I knew I was in trouble. Nurse Looney Tunes said, "We're going to start by making sure the babies are not in distress."

They worked together to attach the fetal heart rate monitoring system to my huge belly, my cough making a difficult job even harder. For the test to be accurate, the equipment must measure the heart rate for each of the babies for at least three uninterrupted minutes, simultaneously. In an ideal world, you can attach one monitor to Baby A and another to Baby B, start the timer and walk away. The trouble is that just after you walk away, one of the babies squirms out of range and the whole test must be started anew.

Trying to be helpful, I said, "I've had several of these tests done. It will go much faster if you each hold a monitor and follow the babies and just get the data you need." Nurse Neon Pink raised an eyebrow. "I'm sorry, I'm not trying to tell you what to do, but I've never had one of these tests last less than 90 minutes unless two people just focus on getting it done."

Perhaps they saw the futility of trying to keep the monitors in place while my body convulsed with coughs, because they quickly resigned themselves to the task. They each pulled up a stool on either side of my bed and focused their attention on chasing squirming unborn babies with fetal heartrate monitors.

I tried to be still as I watched and listened to the monitor. There was Baby A's heartbeat. There was Baby B's heartbeat. And there was another contraction. Trying not to trigger another coughing fit, I whispered, "These aren't real contractions. It's just the stress."

"Well," Nurse Looney Tunes said, "The doctor on duty errs on the side of conservative. She is going to recommend you have a c-section tonight. I won't say any more than that."

She might not have liked me, but in that moment I loved her. Frank and honest nurses are the silver lining in the Modern Medical Machine cloud. I'm not particularly quick on my feet, and she had given me the gift of time to come up with a strategy. While the nurses focused their attention on the babies, I used the quiet to think. I needed to put on my diplomatic charm with the end goal of advocating for myself and my babies.

Other than the wracking cough, I felt strong enough to keep going. My blood pressure was fine, my iron was fine, my proteins were fine. I didn't have discoloration under my eyes or unusual swelling anywhere. I was uncomfortable, as anyone with two babies smashing their internal organs would be, but I was managing. The only red flag was that Baby B wasn't growing as fast as Baby A, and even then there were no signs of placenta failure. The Doppler showed a strong umbilical connection, and Baby B's growth had been steady, if slow.

While the two nurses focused on collecting the data they needed, Will called Midwife Lucy to give her the update and ask for some advice. Midwife Lucy reminded us that doctors don't like to be told what to do, that we needed to give them room to recommend the breathing treatment we all knew I needed.

The data confirmed that the babies were not in distress, and the nurses moved on to other tasks. A doctor checked on me just before ending her shift and ordered a magnesium bolus be administered to slow preterm labor. With the magnesium coursing through my veins, making me warm and flushed with internal heat, I turned on my side to get comfortable and found myself facing the contraction monitor. Although the contractions were subsiding significantly with the help of the magnesium, when I coughed, they increased in intensity and duration. The correlation was strong but after two hours, I had yet to see an internal medicine doctor. The nurses continued to treat me as a woman in labor, and I was getting worried.

A doctor who epitomized the Modern Medical Machine experience I distrusted showed up around 2 A.M. She was almost brutal in her pelvic examination, saying with something like disgust, "You're 1cm dilated." I knew from reading and conversations with other moms that I could have been 1cm dilated for weeks. I knew these measurements to be subjective and I didn't find 1cm to be alarming in the least. But, given her gruff nature, it didn't surprise me a bit when she said, "I suggest we move to a c-section right away."

I was stung, but I was ready for her. Per Midwife Lucy's coaching, I said, "Okay, I understand your recommendation. Do you feel we have tried everything we can to stop the contractions? I mean, is there anything else we can try for my cough first?"

"Well, we could probably try an intensive breathing treatment."

"Okay, could we perhaps give that a go before deciding to move ahead with a c-section?" She agreed and nearly four hours after my admission to the hospital, an internal medicine doctor paid me a visit. The treatment was administered and, as we knew it would, it worked wonders. I stopped coughing and my contractions slowed to one every ten minutes or so, lasting only 30 seconds. I felt the case was clear and that I would be going home shortly.

Around 5:30 A.M., before she went off duty, Dr. Gruff visited me one last time. She did a final pelvic exam and said, "I'm going to debrief the doctor coming on duty and I'm going to recommend you have a c-section today."

I asked, "Have I dilated further?"

"No, you're still at 1cm. But bird in hand. You've carried the babies this far. We may as well take them out now." These were her exact words and it was exactly the attitude that did not make sense to me. So long as the babies were developing well, almost every scientific study showed that longer gestations had better outcomes.

Drawing on another strategy Midwife Lucy had taught me, I said, "Okay. I understand your recommendation. Could I have a few hours to think about it?" The idea is to buy some time to allow a non-emergency situation to unfold a bit. The doctor and I negotiated and agreed that we could give it two more hours to see if the contractions would stop entirely. By then, the new doctor would be on duty and it would be her decision to make. So I tuned out everything around me and started pouring on the hypnobirthing relaxation techniques I'd learned, using imagery and breathing techniques to relax every muscle in my body.

When the new doctor, a small Indian woman with petite hands, arrived, she introduced herself and said, "I understand Dr. Gruff has recommended you have a c-section, and you have until 8 A.M. to think it over. I'm going to endorse her recommendation for a c-section, but also suggest that you be transferred to Clarkesville. I'm concerned about Baby B and I don't want you to be separated from your babies if one needs L3 NICU care. "

New doctor, new negotiation.

"Okay, I understand your recommendation. Could I have another hour to think about this new piece of information?"

"Yes. I'm going to finish my rounds and then we will discuss what to do."

Over the next hour, I would have just one contraction. My fever was gone, my cough was under control and I was able to walk to the bathroom standing more or less upright. It was literally and figuratively the difference between night and day.

When the doctor returned, I pointed out all of this to her.

I said, "I really feel that I am ready to go home."

"Well, I am not comfortable with that. I'd like to transfer you to Clarkesville now."

"But I'm better! I don't want to go to Clarkesville. Clarkesville is for emergencies and this is not an emergency. What would happen if I checked myself out now?"

"You would be considered AMA and your insurance probably wouldn't cover the cost of this visit."

She had me.

Reluctantly, I signed the consent forms to be transferred via a 90 minute ambulance ride to Clarkesville at a cost of $2500.

With remarkable efficiency, a team of nurses and administration staff discharged me into the care of the ambulance team, who lifted me onto a gurney, which they wheeled through the maze of the hospital to the waiting ambulance. I had no personal belongings with me. I wore only a hospital gown. I had a port in my arm and an IV drip for hydration, but other than that, I was naked. They buckled me laying down, and Will followed in our Subaru.

By the time we got to Clarkesville, I was no longer having any contractions. As predicted, the vastly more experienced team of doctors at Clarkesville practically rolled their eyes when they got me checked in.

"Clearly, you are not in active labor. Still, now that you are in our care, we would like to do some assessments of you and the babies."

Our experience at Clarkesville was eye-opening. Here, the doctors, nurses and midwives were more professional, thorough, cheerful and engaged. They agreed that so long as the babies were growing well, they should stay put. They felt that it was best to deliver as naturally as possible, not because it was my wish, but because they were a research-based facility and research shows babies have better outcomes with natural deliveries. They even had nurse-midwives on staff!

After our weekend in Clarkesville, I felt conflicted about my care with Lutheran. I felt a sense of loyalty that came more from habit than from an abiding sense of trust. The nurse-midwives had been supportive of my desire to work with Midwife Lucy, but the one thing I had learned over the course of my pregnancy was that the thing I was shopping for might not be the thing I needed. In something of a mixed blessing, my next appointment with Lutheran made my decision to transfer my care to Clarkesville an easy one. I was scheduled for a regular ultrasound, a tour of the delivery wing, and a fetal heart rate monitoring session. The day was chaotic, the staff seemed stressed and, as usual, everyone was running almost an hour late. I suddenly realized that if I was going to work with the Modern Medical Machine, I wanted to work with the very best that the Modern Medical Machine had to offer.

On the way home from that debacle of a day at Lutheran, I made the necessary phone calls to transfer my care from Lutheran to Clarkesville. That was Thursday. By Friday, they had reviewed my records and called to schedule a visit on Monday. Nobody said anything, but I got the sense they also didn't like the growth difference between the babies.

Throughout my pregnancy with the twins, I asked friends and family to pray that my body would be strong enough to carry the babies 36 weeks, which is considered full-term for twins or, more simply, that the twins wouldn't be born until sometime in July. That coming Monday would make 35 weeks and 6 days of gestation, and I figured that would probably be close enough for the doctors. Over the weekend we mowed the lawn, packed overnight bags, and arranged for care for Cypress and our dog. We left the house very early that Monday, July 1st, hoping, but not really believing, we'd be back before dinner. Twelve hours later I was on the operating table.

SEVEN

C-Section

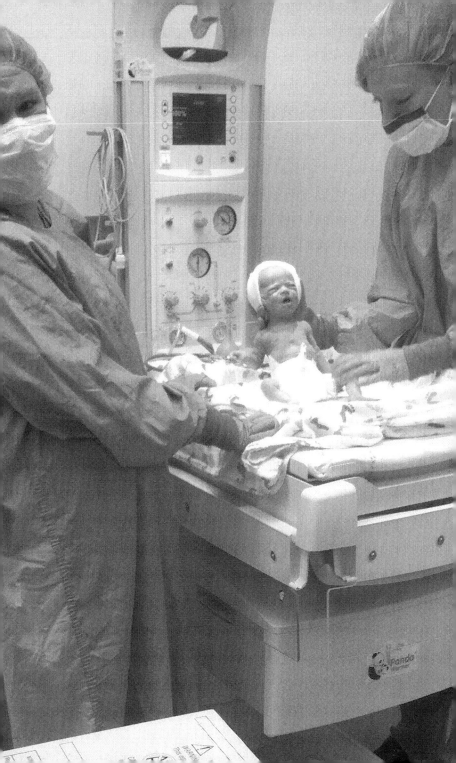

On the count of three, a team of nurses lifted my numb legs onto the operating table, while Tony, the anesthesiologist's assistant, helped guide my chilly torso and huge abdomen into position.

Tony patted my shoulders. "Good?" he asked.

"Yes." *I guess.*

What I had once imagined to be the worst possible outcome of my pregnancy with the twins, short of dying or losing one of my babies, was now a looming reality.

After this operation, I would not be pregnant ever again. I would have three children, but only one experience of giving birth.

Tony moved my arms to "T" position so he could strap them down. The epidural had taken effect and as I dry-heaved over my left shoulder into a pink plastic tub offered by Tony, I could feel the dull tug of nurses adjusting the lower half of my body.

I closed my eyes and began counting backwards.

Ten. I am standing at the top of a stone stairway surrounded by a lush garden. The steps lead down into an inviting cenote.

The air is warm, and from where I stand at the opening of the underground cave, I can see blue-green water beckoning below.

Nine. One step at a time, I descend deeper and deeper into the cave. Soft sunlight filters down through the canopy of trees overhanging the cenote.

Eight. Down, down, down. Past long roots, reaching from their perch above ground through the depths of the cave for a drink of water.

Seven. The temperature is perfect, the air slightly damp on my skin. Sunlight dances on the epiphytes and moss growing on the cave walls.

Six. Deeper, deeper, I sink deeper into the cave. The water awaits my...

"EXCUSE ME!" A woman wearing a blue mask broke into my reverie.

I opened my eyes. In a loud voice, she commanded, "Can you tell me your name and date of birth, please?"

Obligingly, I answered the question for the 50th time that day, "Heather House, ten, thirty, seventy-three."

"Can you tell me why you are here today, Ms. House?"

"I'm here to deliver my twins via C-section."

"And?"

"And to have a tubal ligation," I answered, "So long as you're in there anyway."

Satisfied, she turned away.

Two nurses worked together to erect a curtain across my chest, blocking my view of the surgery. Blocking too, I felt, the surgeon's view of my face. I won't see their work, they won't see my humanity.

The resident doctor peeked over the curtain to remind me that we had met earlier in the day and that she was about to begin the procedure. Her mentor was there to look over her shoulder. I could only imagine what the target looked like. She was aiming for a place on my body that I hadn't seen in months, just above my pubic bone and below the bulging girth my growing babies called home for almost 36 weeks. I asked if she would mind talking through what she was doing so I could feel like a participant in the delivery of my children, a tip I'd picked up just days before by reading the previously neglected chapters on cesarean in my library of birthing books. The resident agreed, but after she said, "I'm going to make the incision now," she never uttered another word to me.

Instead, it was my husband Will who talked me through the procedure, mustering as much gory detail as a Forestry major who is seeing his wife cut open and have babies pulled out of her body can, which is to say that it was a vague, poorly narrated tale punctuated with long pauses ripe with disbelief and sputtering.

I closed my eyes and stood at the top of my cenote. With the warmth of the sun on my skin, I counted backwards from ten once more. The scene was already firmly built in my mind, so I moved through the meditation more quickly.

Ten. I am standing at the top of a stone stairway.

Nine. I begin the descent.

Eight.....

Seven.....

Six....

Five. I descend the final steps to the sandy landing between the stairwell and the edge of the water. I am safe. I am safe. I am safe.

I walked down that same stone stairwell over and over again during the 40 hours I labored with Cypress, and the imagery had the same effect now as it did then: I was transported from a world of fear and pain into a blissfully deep, relaxed state.

Will's voice filtered through my meditation. "Looks like they are making the incision now."

Four. The water is inviting, the temperature perfect. I wade in. My body is loose, relaxed. I feel safe.

So effective is self-hypnosis or, as it's called when used by laboring mothers, Hypnobirthing, there was actually a point during my labor with Cypress that Midwife Lucy asked me to raise a finger when a contraction started and stopped. It was not visible to the outsider that my body was experiencing one minute contractions every three minutes. Just as it was not visible to the team of surgeons and nurses that I was not there on the operating table but, instead, floating in water the color of jewels while they tugged and worked to pull the first baby out.

Now it's Tony's voice I hear. "Is she okay? She is very calm."

Will answered. "She is meditating. She's in her happy place. She's fine."

Three. When the water is up to my chest, I turn to float on my back. Sunrays streak the air. It is silent but for the sound of water dripping somewhere in the back of the cave. My body is free of tension.

A strong tug shifted my whole body a fraction of an inch down the table. Ripped from my skinny dipping daydream, I began to dry heave again. The doctors did not pause in their work and between dry heaves Will said, "The boy is out."

I opened my eyes and looked to the right. Ten feet away, a nurse was holding, or more like dangling, our boy for me to see. He was small, but his limbs were long and his shoulders were square.

An athlete.

Then he was placed on a warming table, one of two set up in the room. A team of nurses crowded around him. Unlike the day that Cypress was born, there was no happy celebration at the sight of a long-awaited baby. No one shed a tear. Not even me.

I wanted to be moved by the sight of my new baby. Instead, I felt nothing. Only a vague sense of disappointment that this was where the journey would end. As much as I wanted to be fully present for the birth of these children in the way that I was for Cypress's birth, I wanted even more for the damn thing to be over with. I tried to prepare myself for the coming hours. *In a few moments, I will be sewn up and the focus will be on Baby B, our girl, who we know is going to be small and who will spend at least this evening in the NICU. Then we'll assess where to go from there.*

There would be no quiet alone time with just my husband and our new babies. There would be no friends to relive the magic of birth with me, sharing victorious recollections of labor and marveling at the mystery. There would be no visits from Midwife Lucy to look forward to. Other than Will, I would never see anyone in this delivery room again. There would be only the numbing efficiency of a hospital crew to whom I owe my and my children's life, even as I begrudge them the privilege of saving it.

I closed my eyes again.

Two. The water laps softly at my shoulders. I float in a state of complete relaxation, utterly content.

One. My mind is still. My body is limp and loose. I am safe.

Will squeezed my hand. "The girl is out."

Again, I opened my eyes to see my baby, but she was whisked away to the other warming table.

I asked Will, "Can you see her? Is she small?"

Will answered reluctantly. "I couldn't really see her. I can't tell if she's small."

The nurses hovered over our girl, just out of my range of view. After a few moments, a strange cry came from the direction of her warming table. It sounded like a kitten. A very angry kitten.

Will asked, "Can we see her?"

The nurses conferred. "Okay, we'll hold her up quick,"

Will readied his cell phone to snap a photo. I craned my neck to catch my first glimpse of my baby girl. She was not pretty, and she was very tiny. I laid my head back down and thought, *This is going to be hard.*

Later, when I look at this first photo of our little girl and her masked nurse, I will be struck hard in the gut by the nurse's eyes, which seem to say, "Oh, she's different, but please try to love this one too." And I will know that this nurse knew that Fern had Down syndrome.

Did everyone in that room know just by looking at her that Fern had Down syndrome? Was it possible they knew before we even started the surgery? Is that why the doctor took so much time with us that morning? He was so charming and kind. Did he see something in the results of the ultrasound that the Maternal Fetal Medicine at Lutheran had been missing all along?

It was time for the tubal ligation. The nurses cared for our babies and Will looked over the curtain to continue his narration. "Wow! They have taken something out of your body and placed it on your belly and…"

"No, stop." I interrupted. "I don't need to hear anymore."

Will smiled at me, his face upside down and sweet. The only person I know who can make a hairnet look sexy. "Okay. I'll let you know when they start sewing you up."

The water supports my body perfectly. I am not pregnant. I am not stretched, bruised or cut open. Nothing hurts. My body feels wonderfully whole, fit and healthy. I am whole. I am safe.

Tony patted my head. "Do you want to touch your baby?"

"Yes."

Convinced I would not try to "help" the doctors with the surgery, Tony unstrapped my hands so I could touch Baby A, my boy. They brought him to me in a bundle and I reached out to touch his downy face. On one side of the curtain, I was a gaping wound. On the other, I was mother to a new baby. Or rather, I was mother to *two* new babies.

Will asked the nurse, "Can I hold him?" She handed our boy to Will, who was so naturally comfortable holding an infant, it made me love him even more.

Nothing about the delivery of our twin babies was how we envisioned it would be. Our birth plan was a joke. The c-section was every bit as horrible as I had feared, but it was over. Now, the cliché was our truth: in the end, we were just happy to have two healthy, normal babies. We would soon be home, adjusting to our "new normal."

My legs are numb and I'm going to be sore, but the worst is over. Baby B is small, but they are going to figure out she's healthy and we'll be home in a couple of days. We've got this.

"Ready to go?" Tony asked. The surgery was complete. In a couple of hours I would meet Fern and my life would slowly start to unravel. But for now, Tony gave me one last pat on the shoulder and I headed back to my room where a few surprises were waiting. Theresa was there, just as happy and fully present for Sylvan as she was with Cypress, and eager to celebrate his victorious birth. Midwife Lucy had arrived while I was in surgery, and she was smiling and saying encouraging things, like, "You're so lucky they let you hold Sylvan on the way back from the operating room." The nurse assigned to watch over me during post-op recovery kept the room lights dim, and she went about her work quietly, giving me time to take in Sylvan and look into Will's eyes to see love and relief. Those moments with Will and Sylvan and our friends were sweet. A gift. The proverbial calm before the storm.

EIGHT

Empowerment and Eating

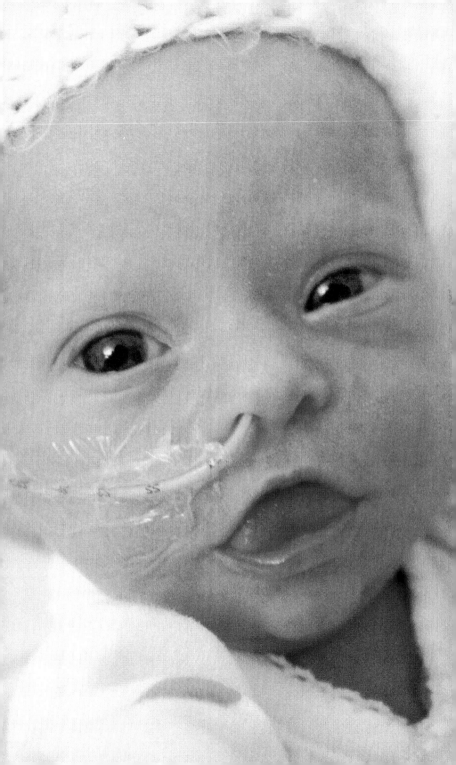

Even though people were staring at my vagina and there was a chance I might poop when I pushed, I found giving birth naturally an incredibly empowering experience.

At least, I *thought* I understood what it meant to feel empowered after birthing my first son at home. The labor was long and hard, lasting the better part of an entire weekend. Supported by friends, guided by a trusted midwife, and doted on by my husband, it was an intimate occasion and together we welcomed a new baby into this world. The most primal of nature's forces flowed through me and I did not fight it; I danced with it. When I first held my newborn baby, Cypress, I felt as though I was meeting both him and myself for the first time. I hardly knew the powerful, sure and graceful person I had become during childbirth. And I liked her very much.

For every feeling of fiery confidence that surged through my body in the days following Cypress's birth, an equal feeling of humiliation and disempowerment chilled me to the bone as I lay spliced open, helpless and dependent on strangers to deliver my twins via a cesarean. What little of my fire still burned deep within was doused when, the next day, Dr. Smith told me she thought my newborn baby girl might have Down syndrome. The world clashed with who I thought I was, and I could not get my bearings. The words "mother of a child with special needs" was like kryptonite to the Superwoman who, just 19 months earlier, had delivered her first born at home.

I never could have guessed that within a few days of being assigned to a role I did not desire, I would come into true empowerment. It happened when I relinquished my ego and stopped defining myself by the number of "wins" I could check off my list and started responding to what my baby really needed for the best possible outcome.

·　　　　·　　　　·

It was a Saturday, Day 6 of Fern's stay in the NICU. Even in the NICU, where tiny babies fresh from the womb are in various stages of fighting for their lives, weekends take on a different, more relaxed vibe. Will and I had made a big decision the night before and we were eager to talk with someone who was familiar with Fern's case. We had been told that her doctor would have the day off and, because it was Saturday, the doctors made their rounds later than usual. I was getting restless. When the team finally rolled up with their individual mobile computer work stations, I was relieved to see among them the smiling face of Diane, the charge nurse who had been with Fern all week.

Fern had been moved to the Level 1 section of the NICU after pacing quickly through Levels 3 and 2, evidence that she was doing very well. She was still an eerie shade of jaundiced green, but managing to keep her level of bilirubin to just within the acceptable range, deftly avoiding light therapy. She was regulating her body temperature without the help of supplemental heat. And, importantly, her heart appeared to be stable. There was a checklist of milestones Fern had to meet before the doctors would release her from the NICU, and she was meeting all but one: Fern was not eating on her own.

Saturday rounds took place in the usual way: the doctors circled up and stared at their screens to read off numbers and notes by way of discussing my baby's progress, never bothering to look at Fern herself. With no new interesting developments, the meeting was quickly over. As the residents rolled off with their carts, I asked Diane for just a minute of her time.

A charge nurse is the person who oversees a unit, managing everything from deliveries, nurse staffing, bed assignments and even phone calls from worried parents. They often play the role of liaison between parents and hospital staff. Diane was good at this job because she had mastery of both logistics and people skills. She was good-natured, competent and professional. She was the kind of woman who exuded dependability with nary an ounce of ego. She remembered details that other people forgot, and she was good at translating doctor-ease into lay language.

"Diane," I said, "Everyone, including you and I, thinks Fern will do better when she gets out of the hospital and goes home. So please tell me honestly," I gave her my best straight-shooter look, "Do you really think we could get Fern out of here in a couple of days? Or was Dr. Smith being optimistic?"

"Well," Diane answered thoughtfully, "Fern *is* doing really well. It's true that Dr. Smith said there was a chance Fern could be out of the NICU by Tuesday, but she absolutely will not send Fern home with a feeding tube. So it really depends on whether Fern starts eating."

"Okay. That's what I needed to hear," I said. "From now on, I want to give Fern a bottle."

For a second, Diane hesitated. Then she asked, "You don't want to breastfeed her?"

Will asked, "Do you think giving Fern a bottle will improve our chances of getting out of the NICU faster?"

Diane caged her answer. "It could." There were, after all, no guarantees.

"Then yes, definitely," I said. "As soon as possible, we want to try giving Fern a bottle."

All week, the NICU staff had done everything possible to support my desire to breastfeed Fern. From the signs on her isolet that read, "No pacifiers. No bottles. I'm learning to breastfeed." to accommodating my groggy 2 A.M. phone calls saying I was running a bit late but would be there to nurse Fern, everyone wholeheartedly supported the system we had in place in hopes that we would succeed.

Several times a day, I set up the NICU privacy screens and tried to nurse Fern. Fern was allotted 30 minutes to eat and, in addition to showing up with the boobs, my job was to record how long she actively suckled. I watched for the muscle in her jaw to lift up towards her ear indicating a good suck and swallow.

Suck, suck suck, suck, suck, s-u-c-k, ssszzzzzzzz.

Did she fall asleep? Yes. Stop timer. Tickle cheek to wake her up.

Suck, suck, s-u-c-k, ssszzzz.

Stop timer. Tickle cheek.

Over and over Fern fell asleep, and over and over I woke her up. At the end of each feeding, I reported to the nurse on duty the total number of minutes Fern actively suckled, which was typically a total of just three or four minutes. Once, Fern nursed for a total of six minutes over a thirty minute session and that was cause for celebration.

A glucose test, which required pricking Fern's heel and bending her foot at an alarming angle to collect blood, was administered just before each feeding and again about 90 minutes after she ate. Fern ate every three hours, so this meant she was being pricked every 90 minutes, around the clock. Pinpricks of dried blood made an entire cosmos of constellations on Fern's tiny heel. Sometimes we got lucky and a pre-feeding prick would still be bleeding ninety minutes later and the painful prick, and accompanying tears, could be avoided.

Adjusting for the calories in the glucose solution being fed to her via IV, we could see Fern was getting *some* nourishment from nursing. But by day three, when infants start to require more complex nourishment, Fern still was not nursing well. So a nasogastric tube, also known as an NG tube, was fed down her nose into her stomach and she began receiving my pumped breast milk via the tube.

I felt conflicted about the NG tube. On the one (pragmatic) hand, it seemed like the logical next step and I was thankful the hospital strongly supported our desire to feed Fern breast milk through the NG tube. On the other, I worried that perhaps Fern wasn't nursing because she simply was not hungry enough to learn. Maybe we were jumping the gun?

Before each meal, the nurse confirmed the feeding tube still led to Fern's stomach (and had not inadvertently shifted into her lungs) by pushing a tiny amount of air through an empty syringe attached to the outer end of the feeding tube. As she did this, the nurse listened with a stethoscope to hear where the air went; confirming it is was Fern's stomach, and not her lungs, that inflated. Then, using that same syringe, the nurse suctioned the contents of Fern's stomach out. If her tummy was empty, it was a sign Fern's digestion was working properly. It might also mean that it was time to increase the amount of milk being fed through the feeding tube. Conversely, if too much milk remained in Fern's tummy between feedings, it could mean that there was either a problem with Fern's digestion, or that we risked overfeeding.

Assured the feeding tube led to Fern's tummy, the nurse then inserted a different syringe containing warm breast milk into the feeding tube. Usually, the syringe containing breast milk would then be placed in a device that automatically slowly compressed the syringe so that the contents were released into the tube entering Fern's stomach through her nose over a 30 minute period. I requested to be allowed to manage the syringe myself. My hope was that if I pressed the syringe during the times when Fern actively nursed, she would get the feedback that swallowing milk meant her tummy felt fuller. The nurses gamely allowed me to experiment.

The syringe contained a single fluid ounce of breast milk, about the same as a travel size shampoo you might get from a hotel. Still, I found I had to fudge and gave Fern a little nourishment when she hadn't sucked in order to empty the contents of the syringe within the allotted thirty minutes. The fact was, when Dr. Smith suggested Fern was doing well enough to go home if she demonstrated she could eat, Fern was still barely nursing.

And that is how it came to be that my first opportunity to advocate for Fern was also an opportunity to release my need to be a certain kind of mother.

I'm a huge proponent of breastfeeding and I cannot understand why anyone would *choose* not to breastfeed. I am pro-choice when it comes to reproductive rights, so I believe that it is ultimately the mother's decision whether or not to breastfeed. Her body, her choice. But science shows that the benefits of breastfeeding a baby are tremendous to both mother and baby. Breast milk is nutritionally superior to and more digestible than every alternative available. It contains immunities to diseases and strengthens a baby's immune system. And, this felt especially important in Fern's case, there have been numerous studies linking feeding formula to lower IQs.

Getting breast milk into Fern wasn't the problem; she was being fed breast milk that I pumped for her via her NG tube. The problem was that I wanted Fern to reap the other less tangible benefits of the act of breastfeeding. Even though the books the hospital provided me about children with Down syndrome lay unopened on the bedside table (it would be weeks before I could bear to read anything about what the future might hold for Fern), I was sure that somewhere in one of those books there was proof that Fern's oral motor skills would benefit from nursing. More than that, I wanted us to bond and to have Fern to know me as a source of comfort. In other words, I wanted to perform what I considered to be one of the most basic of motherly acts of love for my daughter.

Nursing Cypress had come easily. Nursing Sylvan was proving to be even easier. But when it came to nursing Fern, I needed help. Still, I found the persistent attention from the hospital's lactation consultants unnerving. Each time they strolled into the NICU, I started to feel a little defensive. Yes, I wanted all the tips and tricks I could glean from them. But sometimes their attempts at encouragement felt more like pressure to succeed, and I felt like their expectations weren't always grounded in reality.

Fern had a thrusting tongue and lacked oral motor control, both typical challenges of newborns with Down syndrome. Fern was also very tiny. Like a lot of preemies who aren't quite finished baking in the oven, Fern was sleepy. Sylvan was sleepy too, but the kid ate like he was just let out of prison. The cardiologist was pretty sure Fern had a condition called Tetralogy of Fallot, which roughly translates to "five things wrong with the heart," and all the extra work her heart was doing might have been another factor contributing to Fern's lethargy.

Nursing Fern was like solving a problem with half a dozen variables. The solution wasn't straight forward and our attempts at nursing were more like a complex algorithm. I shifted Fern from one position to another while one lactation consultant gently squeezed my breast so milk flowed into Fern's mouth, and another alternately tickled Fern's foot or massaged her cheek to keep her awake while I operated the syringe. But no matter the combination of tricks we used, we could not keep Fern interested long enough to get enough nourishment in her. Unless we had a miracle breakthrough, I didn't think we were going to figure out this nursing thing in the next day or two. I was ready to go home, so I was ready for a new tactic.

First, I had to convince Will that introducing a bottle was the right thing to do. The week had been exceedingly stressful on both of us and, miraculously, we had managed to be kind and loving to each other all week. But I had a sense that Will wasn't going to like the idea of giving Fern a bottle. He has very clear ideas about how he wants to raise his children, and it starts with nursing. I worried we might end up fighting.

That Friday was our first night at the Ronald McDonald House (RMH). The twins were five days old and I was five days post-cesarean surgery. As patients, my room had been located right next door to the NICU, but Sylvan had been banned from entering the NICU. Now that we had been discharged, Sylvan could accompany me to the NICU, but we had to walk across the hospital parking lot and through the maze of the hospital to get to the NICU. Shuttle buses ran regularly during the week, but not after five on Fridays. The distance wasn't great, maybe a quarter of a mile if you included the corridors of the hospital. Unprepared for an extended stay in the hospital, we had no stroller and no baby carrier. In addition to the usual post-cesarean recovery, my cracked rib and aggravating cough made the walk carrying Sylvan tiring. Every time I made the walk between the RMH and the NICU with Sylvan tucked against my body like a football on my forearm, I soaked a maxi pad with post-partum blood.

That night, just back from yet another unsuccessful attempt at nursing Fern, I crawled exhausted into bed. I had just two hours before I needed to nurse Sylvan, pump the other breast and get back to the NICU for Fern's 11 P.M. feeding. I needed to sleep. But when else could I bring up the matter of introducing a bottle with Will?

"Will."

"Hmm???" he answered, already mostly asleep.

"I think we need to give Fern a bottle."

No response, and no way to know what that meant. I guessed he was waiting for me to say more.

"She's just not nursing. She's not even close to figuring it out. I don't really know if she's ever going to figure it out, but she's definitely not going to figure it out by Tuesday."

Will answered, "Okay."

Years of marriage taught me that this was *not,* "okay, let's give her a bottle," but rather, 'okay, say more."

All along, I had the sense that Will did not quite believe I was doing everything I possibly could to get Fern to nurse. He was never antagonist or reproachful, but nursing Cypress and Sylvan was text book easy and it was difficult for Will to understand why it would be any different with Fern. Although he had witnessed a couple of my attempts at nursing Fern, Will usually stayed behind with Sylvan while I went into the NICU. He didn't see how many times the lactation consultants helped me reposition Fern, how I awkwardly held my swollen breast to the mouth of a sleepy baby for 30 minute stretches. Maybe it was because I was postpartum, maybe it was because I considered feeding the babies my "turf," or maybe I was just feeling like a failure, but when Will questioned me about nursing I felt defensive.

"Will," I said, trying not to sound defensive. "Let's just get home. I'm not saying I'm giving up on nursing Fern. But I want to go home and I think giving Fern a bottle might be our ticket out of here."

Silence.

And, uncharacteristically, I did not rush to fill the void.

After a few moments, Will rolled over to face me. "It's your body, and therefore your decision. But I feel sad about it. I really want her to have breast milk…"

I cut him off, irritated. "I'll keep pumping! I'm not saying I don't want to pump!"

"Let me finish, please," he said with a sigh. "I want her to have breast milk, but I also want her to bond with you, with *us*, as easily as possible. I'm just not sure that will happen with a bottle."

If he only knew.

Although it would be months before I gave up trying to nurse Fern altogether, it would only be a matter of days before Will became Fern's primary bottle feeder, giving them ample time to bond in ways that he and Sylvan did not in those early days. Beyond the convenience of Fern taking a bottle to help manage the logistics of feeding twins, Will had "the touch." He could get Fern to polish off a bottle in minutes, with little or no reflux whereas I managed to make her vomit almost every time.

"Will," I said, "I promise you that it will be a lot easier for me to bond with Fern when I can hold her anytime I want to in the comfort of my own home."

It was a point that was hard to argue. Splitting my time between two worlds meant that I had not spent more than a couple of hours at a time with either Fern or Sylvan. Not to mention the fact that I hadn't seen our oldest son, Cypress, in several days. The situation was crushing. Other than the occasional bathroom break or shower, I had held Cypress almost continuously for the first ten days of his life. I wanted to get home so I could experience the luxury of having all three of my kids in one room, on one couch, in one big snuggle.

And so, Will agreed. We would try giving Fern a bottle in hopes of getting back to the mundane, bland existence we loved so dearly.

That morning when we told Diane about our decision, the look that flashed across her face said everything.

"Are you *sure*?" she asked.

Of course she was surprised. Diane knew better than anyone how hard we had worked for nursing. Years of NICU experience had taught her that, with some kids, once they try a bottle they never go back to the breast, preferring the ease of a bottle over the work of the breast. She saw the records and knew I had not missed a feeding all week. Every three hours, around the clock. I was either dedicated or insane. Either way, Diane could appreciate how disappointing it was to be getting nowhere. And yet...I was sure I also detected something like respect in her regard for us.

"We're sure, Diane," I said. "We just want to go home."

"Okay," she said. "I'll change the orders right away."

Will likened what happened next to a whole elaborate system of cogs and fly wheels moving in one direction (everyone supporting our desire to breastfeed Fern) suddenly changing directions as one person after another realized the orders had changed rather abruptly. Amid the confusion of grinding gears, a lactation consultant came around and asked me how things were going.

"Not that great." I told her that we had decided to introduce a bottle. I felt very defensive, but I managed to hold back my prepared argument and waited for her response. She surprised me.

"Aw, I'm sorry," she said kindly, without pity. "I know you gave it your best shot. So did Fern. No one can blame you for wanting to get home, that's for sure."

Oh. Maybe the lactation consultants weren't the pushy hardliners I'd taken them for. Maybe I was projecting my own insecurities on them, my disappointment that things weren't going the way they were supposed to.

As the lactation consultant walked away, I was surprised to find that I felt relieved. And proud. This wasn't about failing to nurse Fern. This was what succeeding at being Fern's mother looked like. My job was to meet Fern where she was, not lament where she wasn't. This was the first of many occasions I have had as Fern's mother to reconsider my own disappointment in what Fern can't do in favor of giving Fern the chance to show me what she *can* do. This setting aside the ego, this letting go of certain expectations, this willingness to let things unfold without constantly judging them to be good or bad, this sense to do what is right for my baby with no thought to what others might think…this is freeing! *This* is empowerment.

At the next feeding, the nurse handed me Fern's first bottle. It was a standard issue clear bottle with a yellow-orange silicon nipple, both of which the hospital considered disposable. Will found the wastefulness so abhorrent he saved all the bottles and nipples Fern used. Thank god he did, because for almost six months, the "disposable" bottles and nipples we saved from the hospital were the only ones Fern could eat from.

I took a seat in the reclining NICU chair next to Fern's bassinet and Will handed her down to me. I positioned Fern in the crook of my left arm and placed a boppy under my elbow for support. Fern was wide-eyed as I offered her the bottle, filled with just over 2 ounces of warmed breast milk. After a questioning pause, Fern did what she had not been able to do all week: she latched and gave a strong suck. A look of recognition and eagerness lit up Fern's eyes. She drank more. It was a sloppy affair, with Fern's tongue loping about, sometimes latching, and sometimes thrusting. Milk drooled down her chin and pooled in the tiny folds under her neck, but there was no question: Fern was eating! She still tired easily and paused often to rest. But she did not sleep and, to everyone's amazement, Fern polished off that first bottle in 7 minutes flat.

And with that, we started making plans to go home.

NINE

Out of the NICU, Into Life

Although Fern's eight days in the NICU were relatively short and uneventful when compared to some of the other more serious cases, the days crawled by for me and I was certain summer, my favorite season, was getting away from us. I was tired of the chilly hospital, tired of worrying about what was wrong with my daughter, tired of being the family who lived at the Ronald McDonald House and ate hospital café food. I vowed that when we got home, we were going to make the most of summer doing the things that make summer memories, like going to the pool and eating from our garden. Fern was released from the NICU on Tuesday and by Friday we were ready for our first adventure out of the house. We headed for The People's Choice Arts Festival, a summer tradition for our family and many of our friends.

I chose to wear a maxi dress, which made the most of my huge boobs and hid my post-partum pooch. Being post-partum hormonal, I was feeling extremely protective of my new babies, especially Fern. So instead of allowing her to be put in the stroller, where strangers might want to reach in and touch her, I insisted on carrying her in my arms, in a football hold. The football hold is a great way to hold a tiny baby, as it supports their whole body and head. I turned Fern belly down on my forearm, her little legs and arms draped on either side of my arms and her tiny head cradled in my hand. Will did the same with Sylvan. Awkward as it may seem, this unconventional position is incredibly soothing to the baby as well as comfortable for the holder.

Almost as soon as we entered the festival, people started to swarm around us. We were completely unprepared for the attention. We held our babies protectively, like we were running backs and the rest of the festival attendees were the opposing team. People stopped in their tracks to ask us, "Are those twins?" And, pointing to Fern in particular, "Is that a real baby?" Others walked purposefully across the open areas between displays to exclaim, "My god, they are so tiny! That one doesn't even look real!" Indeed, with her large eyes and floppy tone, Fern looked a lot like a doll. Fern was tiny and although her skin was still mottled, it was a pretty pinkish white. Only after several minutes of entertaining the usual questions (How much do they weigh? How old are they? Are they identical? What are their names?) we realized that the reason Sylvan wasn't garnering nearly as much attention is because most people have never seen a baby as tiny as Fern, let alone out in public. I was very happy I had thought to hold Fern, as I'm certain people would not have been able to resist touching her. As people ooohed and shook their heads in wonder, I kept thinking, "Can they tell she has Down syndrome? Does she look strange to them?"

As we made our way around the festival, we attracted crowds of 10-20 people every time we stopped. At one point, a gentleman dragging a woman behind him came walking purposefully up to me. He tugged at his wife's hand. "Look at this Diane, look at this baby!" Diane made appropriate remarks like, "Oh, isn't she cute," but she wasn't nearly as taken with Fern as the man. He was clean-shaven and nicely dressed. Unlike us, he looked like someone who could actually afford to purchase some of the art at the festival, not just the funnel cakes. He turned to me with wonder in his eyes, "I met you over there," pointing towards the forager's tent in the far corner, "And I just had to show my wife your babies. I have never seen such small babies, especially this one!" After he walked away, I turned to Will with tears in my eyes and said, "People can't help themselves because Fern isn't supposed to be here. She's defying everyone's expectations. Babies this tiny are supposed to be in the hospital."

It was the first time I had an appreciation for how Fern was going to blow everyone's expectations out of the water. In addition to whatever else she may or may not have been, Fern was *strong*. Barely ten days old and she had already been through so much. Because she was tiny, people assumed she was also fragile and weak. This was just the beginning of people being wrong about Fern.

One of the reasons I wanted to attend the festival, a place where we were sure to run into dozens of people we know, was to engage in the conscious act of claiming Fern as my own. When I saw the wonder in the gentleman's eyes, the lump in my throat told me the scales were starting to tip a little. I wasn't only feeling sadness about Fern. I was starting to feel proud, too. Fern had gotten herself out of the NICU in record time and I was her Mama. Already, we were a force to be reckoned with.

Just as we were leaving the festival, we passed a thirty-something year-old woman who had Down syndrome. She was holding hands with a woman I presumed was her mother.

She was overweight, very short, poorly dressed and had a rather vacant look on her face. My heart sunk and I started to shed tears behind my sunglasses. This was my nightmare. I could not imagine my Fern growing up to be like that, needing me to hold her hand when she was 30 and I was, what, 70? Were we doomed to be a case of the infirm leading the pathetic?

Breathe. Enjoy your baby. You can figure out tomorrow when tomorrow comes.

•   •   •

The People's Choice Arts Fest is an annual milestone for me now, a sort of informal anniversary marking how far Fern and I have come. Just after Fern and Sylvan's first birthday, I saw a woman who had Down syndrome at the arts festival and I made a beeline for her to introduce myself. She was there with her well-heeled family and gorgeous sister. Her name was Ally, and we shook hands and I took off my sunglasses to make eye contact. Instead of seeing a list of problems or future disappointments, I saw a woman who had personal tastes, lifelong goals and a unique personality. Someone who was an important member of a healthy, loving family. Yes, her face did look a bit vacant as I approached, but she lit up for our introduction and was entirely engaged in our conversation. I wasn't afraid of her or worried whether Fern would grow up to be like her. I just wanted to get to know her.

I never would have guessed that the following year, just two years after weeping under my sunglasses thinking of my dreadful future as an old lady having to hold hands with my grown daughter with special needs, I would be glad to run into adults who have Down syndrome at the People's Choice

Festival, people I know by name. We high-fived like old friends and they gave the update on jobs and new challenges, like learning to navigate the public transportation system. There I was smiling easily, curious and eager for whatever little bits about their lives they might be willing to share with me. I was practically breathless in my desire to get closer, to know as much as possible, greedy for insight on what the future might hold.

TEN

Does Your Little Girl Have Down Syndrome?

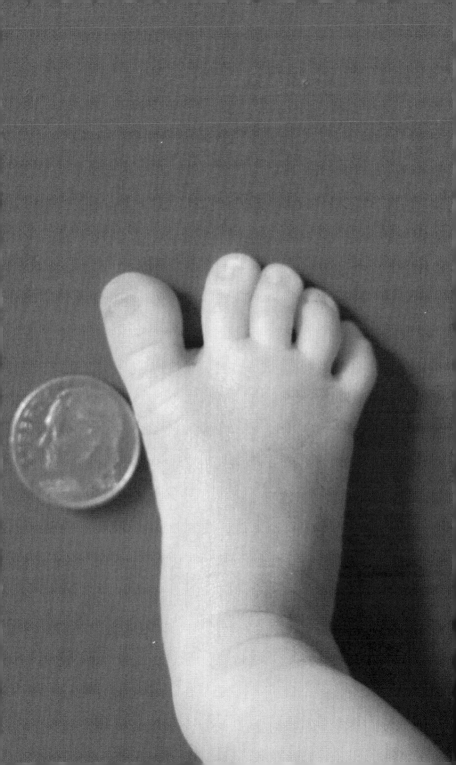

There are a few milestones specific to the parent of a child with special needs. There's the time you announce to your community of friends and family that your child has a diagnosis. There's the day you wake up and realize that your child's diagnosis isn't the first thing on your mind, that life is going to return to being mundane after all. And there's the first time you ask a total stranger whether their child has the same diagnosis as yours.

So when I first noticed the little girl sitting in the red stroller, I took my time in assessing her. There was no hurry, as she was engrossed watching the bearded man wearing a tall striped hat do quarter tricks with his monkey.

We were at The 139th Annual Centre County Grange Encampment and Fair, which I affectionately call the "Gross Encroachment" due to the massive number of people who descend on our tiny town for ten days to camp out and consume huge quantities of deep fried food. Grange Fair has all the entrapments of a typical county fair, including second tier country bands, tractor pulls, a fairway of rides, FFA show animals and muddy alleys that, like the arteries of the people who walk them, are clogged with greasy food.

And we are not one bit above it. We attend annually to consume our fill of fried dough and gawk at the general public. And now that we have children, we travel with quarters for the man with the monkey.

Will was helping Cypress hand Mr. Monkey Man a quarter when I noticed the girl. She had big bright eyes and blonde pigtails. She seemed like any other kid, except…what was it? Perhaps it was the bridge of her nose or the circles under her eyes that made me I wonder if she maybe had Down syndrome. Or maybe it was the way her mouth was hanging open, just a little. Fern was just a few months old and I had never approached a complete stranger about whether their child had Down syndrome, but this seemed like my next mothering milestone. The thought of approaching the family made my adrenaline rush with fear, but I was desperate to connect with them.

I looked away from the girl and focused on Mr. Monkey Man, who was explaining that Cypress had to hold very still so the monkey could give him a kiss. Not yet two, Cypress was too squirmy for the monkey's taste. At a quarter a trick, Mr. Monkey Man had to keep the show moving if he was going to break minimum wage, so Cypress had to settle for a high-five from the monkey. Cypress gave me and his dad a big smile, and I turned my attention back to the little girl.

It was Friday night, the busiest night of the fair and even though there were throngs of people threading past the loose circle that formed around Mr. Monkey Man, my entire attention was focused on this girl. I was looking for a sure sign that she had Down syndrome. I noticed her sparkly princess pink shoes and found what I was looking for: confirmation by way of "sandal toe," the tell-tale space between the big toe and the second toe that almost all people with Down syndrome have.

Now what?

It's not like I had to *do* anything. I was certain that neither of the little girl's parents had noticed me staring at her, though her older brother had and was showing signs of feeling a little protective. Part of me wanted to nudge Will and say knowingly, "Look, she's one." But subtleties are completely lost on Will and I knew I'd have to spell it out for him. He'd gawk and smile at her, and then I'd have to say, "Don't stare!"

Instead, I decided to approach her mother on my own. I wanted to say, "Hey, we have something in common." But I was terrified. Not usually a shy person, it wasn't my personality holding me back. It was something much bigger, much deeper. In some respects, this was the first of many rites of passages that I would go through in my quest to claim my daughter as my own, and reclaim the parts of me that I still liked about me. And it scared the hell out of me.

Why does this have to be such a big deal?

When I first started taking Cypress on outings as a newborn, I could chat up a perfect stranger for 20 minutes about the lack of sleep, the color of my baby's poop, and the pros and cons of nursing bras without ever making a proper introduction. All we had to have in common was that we were mothers of newborns. What made this so different?

A little boy who looked to be about ten froze in place while the monkey gave him a kiss on the cheek, and Mr. Monkey Man was on to the next customer.

"Heather? You ready to go?" Will asked.

Now or never.

"Not yet." I answered.

Shit.

With the rake of three fingers, I swooped back the bangs of hair that had come loose from my barrette and pinned them with the other hand.

What's the worst that can happen?

I retrieved the tinted lip balm from my jeans pocket and casually applied a layer.

Maybe she'll be really pissed off and I'll just end up making a fool of myself.

Then I dug in the corners of my eyes to remove eye boogers and dragged my index fingers beneath the bottom lid to wipe away any mascara smears.

Or maybe she'll be so embarrassed she'll just walk off.

Will looked at me over his shoulder. The twins were getting restless in their stroller.

"I just need a minute," I said, without offering an explanation.

What if she's mean? What if all the moms in the Down syndrome club are mean??

I started to face the little girl's mother and suddenly tears began to well up in my eyes. I turned away again.

What kind of person blubbers all over a perfect stranger at the county fair??

I worked to force my tears back. Fumes from funnel cake scented oil wafted over me, sweet overtones mingling with the salty smell of sweat dripping from under my bra line. I meant to take a deep slow breath, but all I could manage was a quick, noisy inhale and a windy exhale.

Okay, just go already.

Just as I turned to the little girl's mother, I felt the surge of nerve I have when I know I must summon the courage to do the impossible. I have felt this surge on just two other occasions. Once, when I was a novice mountain biker facing an extremely steep descent, in the split second before I released the handbrake and careened down the hill, I felt the rush of courage surge through my frozen body and move me into action. And once, when I was prepared to kill a maggot-infected chicken with my bare hands to put it out of its misery, I experienced a wave of sureness take over my movements, overriding the doubts and fear in my brain.

I closed my eyes and envisioned myself doing the impossibly scary task before me.

Ready......

Set.......

(Now the surge of electric nerves)

GO!!!!

Once more, I turned to the mother of the little girl in the red stroller.

"Excuse me," I said, willing myself to look at her, worried that I might see something about myself reflected back, something that marked us both as mothers of children with Down syndrome. Sadness? Hopelessness? Self-pity?

"Yes?" she answered, looking perfectly normal in all respects. She was pretty, with the same blue eyes and blonde hair as her daughters. She cut a cute figure in tight denim capris and a red baby tee with the local country music station logo emblazed across the front.

Say it. Just SAY it.

The words caught in my throat. Just seven weeks post-partum and just seven weeks after receiving the shock of my life, I was hardly in control of my emotions on even a good day. Now, as I was about to "come out" with my new status of "Mother of a child who has Down syndrome," my trembling lips betrayed my nervousness.

Unsure and afraid, I let the surge carry me and asked, "Does your little girl have Down syndrome?"

"Um, yeah?" the woman answered cautiously as she reached out to stroke a blonde pigtail.

Relieved that her reaction was calm and friendly enough, I flashed a big smile. I scooped up Fern from the stroller and proudly held her up, practically "WHOOP-ing," as if I'd just won the giant stuffed panda at the Skee-Ball tent.

"So does mine!" I said. "This is Fern!"

ELEVEN

Learning from the Best

As the word spread about our newest family members, people asked whether we had met the Smith family who, like us, has a set of twins: one of whom has Down syndrome and one who does not. Naturally, I tracked the Smiths down and invited them to dinner. At the time, our twins were just a couple of months old and the Smith twins were in their 20's.

Like our twins, Adam and Meredith are as different as they can be. Meredith is quiet, reserved, and sweet. Adam is outgoing, friendly, and he has Down syndrome. I immediately picked up on Adam's sense of individuality and style because he had glasses that looked fantastic on him and he was sporting long hair that would give even McDreamy a run for his money.

Turns out, Adam is a bit of a McDreamy himself. I had asked whether either of them had a serious relationship. Meredith said no, and Adam told us a bit about his *current* girlfriend. Apparently, Adam has had numerous girlfriends. In fact, his father shared that one year Adam had three different girlfriends (at three different times…no scandalous cheating here!) in the same class, which made for a rather uncomfortable school year.

Later when I asked him whether there was ever a time he felt like he needed to stand up for himself, Adam told me about a summer at Boy Scout camp when some of the guys were giving him a hard time. Adam had to tell them that it wasn't cool to pick on him because he had Down syndrome. He went on to say that it had been hard to make friends with the boys. Needling him a little, I said, "Yeah, I'm sensing you like girls a lot better." Without missing a beat, Adam laughed and with a little playboy pride said, "You got that right!"

To share a laugh with Adam is to know with deep satisfaction that this thing with Fern is going to be alright. I love to talk and I love to laugh, and I desperately want to be able to do both with my girl. Spending time with Adam gave me great hope.

Adam and Meredith were both forthcoming and helpful. They shared their dreams (she wants to be an engineer, he wants to be a rock star) and the conversation felt authentic to me. No one was patronizing Adam by "including him." He was just another adult at the table marveling at the unique and rich experience of life.

At one point I asked the twins, "So, what do you think your parents did right?" Adam sat up straight and burst out, "I LOVE this question!" before confirming what I'd begun to suspect. Adam and Meredith's parents see them as individuals, not diagnoses. Mr. and Mrs. Smith have made a practice of helping their kids identify their passions (whether it is a strength or not) and giving them the tools they need to pursue them.

Before their arrival, I mentally made a list of questions I wanted to ask the Smiths. As curious as I was about what it would be like to parent a child with Down syndrome, and what it would be like for Fern to have Down syndrome, the opportunity to ask questions of the twin of a person with Down syndrome was what I was most looking forward to. What did this all mean for Sylvan, my beautiful, developmentally "normal" baby boy?

But what was striking to me about our conversation was the number of questions I never got around to asking. Like, "Was there a time when you felt ashamed of your brother?" And, "Do you ever feel jealous about the things your sister can do that you cannot do?" These questions never came up because the answer was obvious: "YES! Duh!" We're talking about HUMAN BEINGS here! These are feeling that almost all siblings have, irrespective of whether one of them has Down syndrome or not.

It's obvious that Adam and Meredith were raised in a healthy family and, whatever incidences they may have had in the past, the overall impression you got of the relationship between the twins was of love, respect and deep caring for one another. That this kind of relationship was possible between twins, so different as mine, was a welcome revelation.

TWELVE

I Love Zoloft

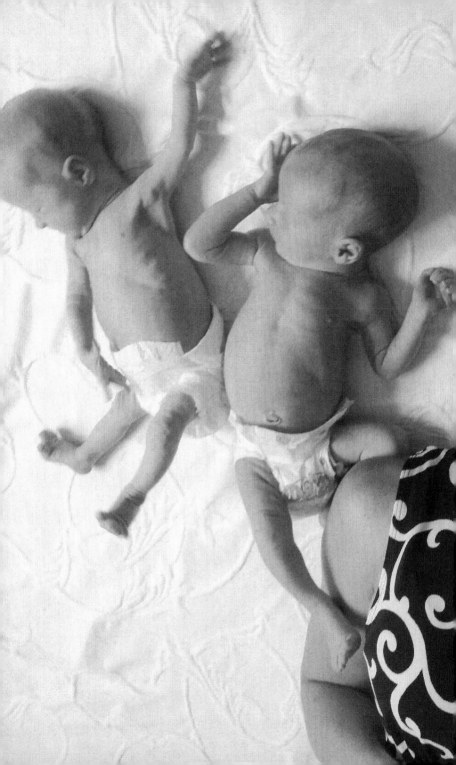

When I sat across from Helen, my therapist, it was my habit to stare out the second story window of the old house-cum-therapist-office as I rummaged through bits of my brain and soul in search of honest answers to probing questions. I'd study the Swiss-inspired trim of the old-house-cum-student-apartments across the street or absently notice people crossing the road as I pushed myself for the truth of what was bugging me.

Today, I had a question for Helen. I was barely settled on the loveseat directly across from Helen's oversized arm chair before I blurted, "So, Helen, is my life hard? I mean, you see a lot of people. Am I just a pansy?"

Helen lowered her mug to rest on her lap. Her legs were folded beneath her and her long flowy skirt was tucked neatly around them. She gave me an earnest and gentle smile. "You're not a pansy," she said. "Unquestionably, your life is hard."

I needed her reassurance. Or maybe I was seeking her permission. "Can you say more on that, please?"

"Heather," she said, "you are just a few months into this new paradigm of having a child with special needs. You have three kids under the age of two. From what you have told me, finances are tight and you don't have any family who lives close by to help. You haven't slept for more than three hours straight in who knows how long and now, today, you tell me that Fern, who doesn't even weigh seven pounds, is going to have open heart surgery?" Helen closed her eyes and gave an exaggerated nod. "Yes. Believe me. What you are doing is hard."

For the first time since we'd started working together, I cried. "Okay, then. That's what I needed to hear," I said. "I think I need to go on some kind of antidepressant."

Helen gave me a steady look. "I think that would be an excellent idea."

●   ●   ●

I knew my life could be a whole lot worse, that things could be a lot harder for me and Fern. From our trips to the hospital, I knew that some of the ordeals people faced made Fern's openheart surgery look like a game of Operation. Still, I just could not find the straps on my boots by which to pull myself up. And even though I knew it to be a waste of energy, I despised myself for being sad and angry all the time.

"Is this the first time you have struggled with depression or anger issues?" Helen asked.

"No," I answered. "Anger seems to be my default emotion."

"Have you ever been on any kind of prescribed antidepressant before?"

"No. I usually just exercise more or drink St. John's Wort."

"So what's different for you this time?"

I looked out the window just over her right shoulder and focused on the yellow leaves in the tree brushing against the building. "I don't actually know that it is any different. I mean, anger is anger and I have always struggled with it on some level. The problem is now I have three kids and I'm losing my shit on them."

"And you don't want to be angry with your kids?"

"No, it's horrible. Like when Sylvan wakes up screaming in the middle of the night, I get so mad I want to throw him against the wall." I looked at her make sure she knew I was being dramatic. "You know what I mean. I don't *really* want to throw them against the wall. But I understand why the hospital made us watch that stupid video about not shaking the baby."

"What do you do in those moments?"

"Well, last night I put myself in a timeout." It had been a rough night. Sylvan woke up screaming and, deliriously tired and disoriented, I scooped him up and offered him my breast. He would not nurse. So I sat up and put him over my shoulder. He would not burp. I checked his diaper, and it was dry, not too tight. I swaddled, shhh-ed and swung him sideways, but nothing seemed to help. Sylvan's shrill cry simultaneously awakened in me a primal panicked need to soothe him and a deep loathing for being the one assigned to this role. My teeth clenched and I fought back tears of frustration.

The rational voiceover from the video played in my head: *Don't shake the baby. A baby is safer crying in the crib than crying in the arms of a frustrated person who might harm them.*

So I put Sylvan next to Fern in the No-Sleeper (our affectionate nickname for the co-sleeper pushed up against our bed) and locked myself in the bathroom. But the heat of boiled blood laced with wasted adrenaline still coursed through my veins. Frustrations like this were piling up and taking a timeout was like sticking a piece of gum in the gaping hold of the Titanic. I was sinking, and fast.

"And is it just the nights that are bad for you?"

"I wish." I didn't mean to sound snide, but I honestly didn't know which was worse, the long nights of breastfeeding and pumping, or the long days when I was home alone with three children under the age of two.

After months of sleep training, it seemed the only thing Fern and Sylvan could agree on was that one of them should be awake at all times, usually crying. It was nearly impossible to just relax and hold a baby for cooing and cuddling, the way I did with my first born. With Cypress, I could just stare and stare at him, marveling at the wonder of his being. But, with the twins, I frequently had to set aside whomever I was holding to tend another need, which inevitably meant that baby would also be upset. I finally realized that if both the babies and Cypress were awake it was easier to not hold anyone, but to just sit on the couch quietly, like a tiger in waiting, until someone needed something. I would jump up, settle a baby or tend to a need, then sit back down and wait. It was a hellish game of Baby Whack-A-Mole.

"And how is Cypress fairing in all of this?" Helen asked.

The image of Cypress's face crumpling when I yelled at him that morning came in a flash. I started to cry again. "He's just so small and innocent. Every time I get mad at him, I see a piece of his world is destroyed. He's crushed." I reached for another tissue and worked my way through that awkward moment when you have to blow your nose in front of your therapist. "I can see that he doesn't know if he can trust me. I'm his mom! I'm the one person he is supposed to be able to trust in this world!"

"It sounds like you feel guilty for being angry with Cypress."

"Yeah, we used to have a really special relationship. Every time I get mad at him, I'm afraid it will never be the same again."

Poor Cypress. Never was there as sweeter, more rational little guy. At 19 months old, he stepped into his role of Big Brother with the grace and strength of a true leader. By 22 months old, his once mostly-kind mother must have seemed like a different person entirely. I certainly did not feel like myself.

It was one thing for Cypress to be crushed when I yelled at or spanked him. It was quite another, and more worrisome, that he was starting to show signs of just accepting that I was a hotheaded mom.

"I just need to figure out how to model kindness for my kids, or they are going to turn out to be jerks like me. My parents were angry a lot, and I was terrified of them. I want to do better for my kids."

"And so what have you been trying this time?" she asked.

"Well, I'm doing what I can. No caffeine. Taking the occasional walk. Trying to eat right. It's just hard. Mostly what I need is sleep and, with the twins nursing every three hours, that's not easy to get."

"Do you think you would be a better mom if you got more sleep?"

"Definitely, but that's not going to happen. Not so long as I insist on giving Fern breastmilk."

Before the twins were born, I read about a model that a lot of nursing mothers of twins use to get more sleep. The idea is that mom goes to bed when the twins go to bed, around dinnertime for most folks. Then dad feeds the twins a late-night bottle while mom sleeps. By the time mom gets up for the next feeding, she should have slept six whole hours!

It didn't work like that in our house. I pulled the blackout curtains and went to bed with the twins right after dinner, when the summer sun was still shining brightly. But I could never produce enough milk and I was often pumping the very bottle Fern was ready to drink, so I had to get up for the late-night feeding. There are plenty of studies that link feeding formula to lower IQs and, in Ferns case, IQ points are at a premium. Every night, I felt like I had to make a choice between getting sleep, which I desperately needed, and providing the nutrition my baby needed for the tiniest leg up in this competitive and cruel world.

"Is there a babysitter you can call so you can nap?"

These were all good questions. Neither Will nor I had family close, but we didn't lack community. After the twins were born, people came out of the woodwork to lend support. In just six weeks, we had over 100 visitors. Three months later and we still had a steady stream of visitors. Everyone wanted to hold the tiny babies and they often came bearing food and gifts for Cypress as well.

I had mixed feelings about all the visitors. I'm an extrovert and also a much better mom when I have witnesses, so I usually welcomed the company. And the twins rarely synced up for me to take a nap anyway, so company was a nice distraction. But every so often, a visitor might arrive when all the babies were sleeping and I would forfeit a nap out of politeness.

"It sounds like you have given this a lot of thought and you're doing everything within your power to be healthy. If you want to go on an antidepressant, you just need to see your doctor."

Within 48 hours of starting the lowest dose of Zoloft, I noticed a difference in how I felt. It was amazing. I was me, only better. Likeable. Almost patient. There was a noticeable pause between an event that triggered me, like being awakened by what sounded like banshees screaming in the middle of the night, and my reaction to that event. And in that pause, I had time to decide what action to take. This was the difference between acting on my impulse (which inevitably was to get pissed off and yell at someone, maybe even kick a wall) and acting with purpose, maybe even compassion. With Zoloft, I found a mental state I never knew I had, one that could witness the ups and downs of life with a certain detachment, without acting on every emotional response that came up. Without taking life so goddamned personally. Best of all, I saw that I had an opportunity to rebuild the trust between me and Cypress. The anger subsided and, with it, the self-loathing.

Right away, I decided I would be very open about being on antidepressants. This was a miracle drug and I couldn't understand all the shame around using it. When I told my natural healer friends that I was on antidepressants, they wanted me to assure them that I'd already tried everything else. Yes, I've been drinking chamomile tea. Yes, I avoid caffeine. Yes, I'm trying to get outside for some fresh air every day. No, I'm not getting enough sleep. No, I don't have time or money to go get a massage.

When I complained about the torturous combination of sleep deprivation and post-partum hormones (I would have confessed to killing your grandmother if I thought it would buy me a whole night's rest), fellow earth mamas bemoaned my decision not to save the placentas from the birth of our twins. So sleep deprived was I, my body actually ached and vibrated until I thought I would vomit, and these mamas thought maybe I wouldn't be experiencing these symptoms and dramatic mood swings if I had encapsulated the placentas for consumption. Meanwhile, I consider NOT eating placenta a great control for postpartum depression because, no matter how bad things seemed, I could always say to myself, "Well at least I'm not eating my placenta."

Even my own husband, who witnessed and was often the target of my regular rampages, had considerable misgivings about me going on antidepressants. He was disappointed and maybe even scared for me. Like a lot of people, I think Will consider it a cop out to take a prescription medicine for emotional issues and I think he worried I might be looking to numb feelings when I should actually be engaging and trying to grow from them. He felt guilty for not making enough money to pay for a babysitter, but did that mean I was going to need to be on antidepressants my whole life? Will knew I was bearing the brunt of sleep deprivation so he could function at the office, so did that mean I could go off the antidepressants when I started getting more sleep?

In the end, I didn't care what other people thought. This was a new chapter in my life, one where I felt confident caring for my mental health and knew with absolute certainty that I would do anything if it meant responding to my kids with kindness instead rampages. I wasn't about to add "other people's opinion of me" to my list of worries. "Listen," I told them, "I take an anti-inflammatory for my hip pain, an anti-histamine for my allergies and now an antidepressant for the rest of it."

My mom was among the people who were a little uncomfortable with me going on antidepressants. Or maybe it wasn't so much that I was taking antidepressants, but that she wondered whether I really had to talk about it all the time. Once, she overheard someone pay me a parenting compliment and she kind of flinched when I said, "Thanks! Zoloft has really changed my life!"

But then she came to stay with me for a week to help while Will was out of town. It was a typical week, full of doctor appointments, visits from Fern's therapists and general running around. At the end of a long day, which included a stop at the pharmacy to pick up my beloved prescription, I asked her to help me get the kids ready for bed. I was refilling my days-of-the-week pill box as she struggled to get Cypress, a squirmy and restless toddler, into his PJ's.

Plink, plink, plink, the little blue pills of patience dropped into place and snap, snap, snap I closed the lid on each of the seven tiny boxes. Instead of focusing on the task of getting his feet into the legs of his pajamas, Cypress watched me, distractedly holding on to my mom's head for balance and pushing her dyed-red hair into her eyes.

"Cypress! Pay attention," she said. "Put your foot in your jammies!"

Cypress turned and, instead of stepping into the pajamas, he kissed my mom on the nose, lost his balance and fell into her lap for the third time. I knew she was finally getting a taste for what my days were like when, frustrated and tired, she looked up at me with woeful eyes and said, "Could I have a couple of those?"

THIRTEEN

Fall

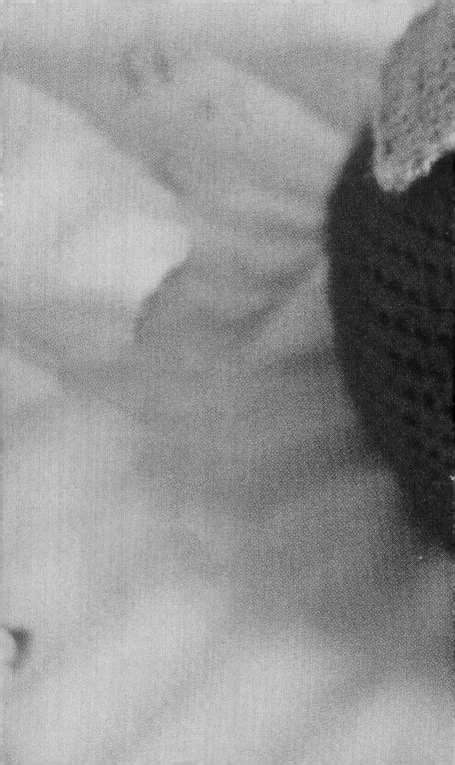

Fall came and, with it, and our annual Halloween-birthday celebration.

When you're dressed like a cat and the phone rings at nine o'clock at night, the last person you want it to be is your child's cardiologist.

"Hello?" I answered, adjusting my fuzzy ears to accommodate the phone.

"Yes, hello, Ms. House."

I recognized the voice instantly.

"This is Dr. Ahmad. I am sorry to be calling so late."

"Hi Dr. Ahmad." Our dinner guests went silent around the dining room table. Everyone knew we were waiting to hear from Dr. Ahmad. "No problem," I said as I moved to the bedroom, closing the door behind me.

I sat on the bed. "I don't like getting calls from doctors this late because it's never good news," I teased.

The last time a doctor called us after hours was to tell us that our daughter Fern had hypothyroidism and would need to be medicated for life.

"Yes, well, I'm afraid it's not great news," Dr. Ahmad said. "You see, I reviewed Fern's case with the other doctors today and we were not able to come to an agreement about whether Fern is a good candidate for the heart surgery at this time." He sounded truly sorry. "Unfortunately, it is not clear from the echocardiogram whether the hole in her heart is significant enough to warrant an intervention. I'm afraid Fern was moving too much during the echo."

No surprise there. Fern screamed and squirmed during the entire echocardiogram and I had been warned that the results might not yield good data.

Just then, I caught a glimpse of myself in the mirror. Black ears poked out of my mousey-brown hair, painted whiskers animated my naturally pointy nose, and pink cat-eyed glasses masked sleep-deprived hazel eyes. It was my 40th birthday, the day before Halloween, and now that the kids had gone to bed, I was the only one dressed in costume.

I put on my mature, concerned mother voice. "Okay, where do we go from here?"

Dr. Ahmad explained that the hole in Fern's heart was not so big that surgery was the obvious answer, but it was large enough that we needed a better echocardiogram.

Dr. Ahmad said, "I'd like you to take Fern to Clarkesville for a sedated echocardiogram. The team has agreed on the circumstances under which we will recommend whether to go ahead with the surgery or wait. Dr. Morris will conduct the echocardiogram and she will be able to tell you more once she has the results."

"Okay," I said, because it sounded like a reasonable plan and, really, what else could I say? I certainly could not share the irrational thought going through my head. *Just schedule the damn surgery already. The insurance deductible is paid. Let's just get this over with so we can move on.* What kind of mother would wish an open-heart surgery on her four-month-old baby? It seemed cruel of me. Looking back, maybe it was my way of grasping for control in a situation that felt completely out of control.

Since the day Fern was born, we had been caught in the bowels of the Modern Medical Machine. As an example, when Fern didn't pass a hearing test at the hospital, we went to one audiologist, and then another, to determine whether she couldn't hear or her inner ear was just too small for the equipment to work properly. We even made a special 3 hour trip to the Down syndrome Clinic in Pittsburg with no conclusive results. Meanwhile, we knew she could hear. She was responsive, alert and engaged. Frustratingly, one ear always passed the hearing test, but it was never the same ear two times in a row. To this day, at almost 3-years-old, Fern has never passed a hearing test in both ears on the same visit. And yet, what better proof do we have that Fern hears just fine than the fact that she talks better than most kids who have Down syndrome in her age group? Still, who wants to be the mom who doesn't schedule the recommended follow up test, no matter how unnecessary it may seem?

While I might roll my eyes when the audiologist recommended a follow-up, I had no idea what to make of the cardiologists recommendations. To me, it seemed that if the hole in Fern's heart was truly a critical issue, it would be obvious. But it was more complicated than that. Dr. Ahmad explained that while the issue may not be life threatening, we could be at a critical juncture for heading off further complications, like pulmonary hypertension, which would be irreversible.

So, while Will went to work, keeping us all housed, fed and clothed, I took on the full-time job of managing Fern and all of her appointments, sometimes as many as three in one week. I didn't want to complain, and yet it was no small matter getting Fern, her twin, and their two-year-old brother into the car and out the door. I was ready to transition from playing the role of Fern's manager to simply being Fern's mother.

Logistics aside, I felt like we were living in limbo, waiting to get on with our lives. Surgery would almost certainly result in a setback for Fern. Therapists warned that she might experience a regression of the milestones she had already met, like being able to hold her own bottle, and milestones yet to be me,t would be pushed even further off into the distance. The sooner we put the surgery behind us, the sooner we could get Fern back on track.

Dr. Ahmad continued, "The reason I am calling you so late is because there happens to be an opening to do a sedated echo at 7 A.M. on Friday morning."

It was Wednesday night and I suddenly felt very happy that I did not act on my impulse to die my hair pink for my 40th.

Dr. Ahmad said, "I know it is short notice, but the next opening isn't for two weeks. Can you make it?"

"Of course, we'll make it work," I said.

And then he dropped another bomb. "I'm sorry, Ms. House, but because Fern is so small, she will be required to stay in the hospital overnight for observation."

Oh goodie. That meant another night at the Ronald McDonald House for the rest of the family.

Dr. Ahmad told me his assistant would be in touch with more details, then we hung up and I returned to our dinner party. The smells of our late meal still lingered even though the dinner plates had been cleared and, in their place, mugs of hot tea steamed on the table. Everyone looked up at me expectantly, and Will came to stand beside me. My eyes filled with tears and, feeling stupid and hating my cat costume, I said, "They want to sedate Fern to get a better look at her heart."

• • •

The anesthesiologist warned us that it's not uncommon for kids with Down syndrome to take a while to respond to sedatives and he explained that he had cooked up a cocktail of sedatives, specially formulated to take into account the difference between nerve receptors of a typical individual and those of an individual who has Down syndrome.

To me, the procedure seemed relatively uneventful, if predictably disturbing. Fern was calm while the nurse took great care in finding a vein for the intravenous needle. She hit her mark the first time and was visibly relieved. Having seen a number of nurses fumble with Fern, Will complimented her and she confessed that she hadn't worked with such a tiny baby in a long time. At four-months-old, Fern barely weighed 7 pounds.

The team of nurses and doctors must have known what it was like for a parent to turn their baby over for sedation the first time, because they allowed me to stay by Fern's side to sing and coo to her until she was nearly out. In the coming months, Fern would be sedated several times, but we were never asked to stay for the procedure again. I guess if you've seen one baby-sedation you've seen them all. As Fern drifted off, we were escorted to a waiting room.

Within two hours, we had our answer. Dr. Morris invited us to join her at a table in the waiting room where she produced an ordinary piece of notebook paper with an image of a heart sketched by hand.

"Fern did great," she said. They always start with something positive before giving you the bad news.

"Unfortunately, the hole is bigger than we originally thought. It is also located much closer to the valve than we originally believed it to be." Dr. Morris used her pencil to point to the place in Fern's heart where a hole was allowing blood to flow backwards, thereby skipping the important step of getting oxygenated by the lungs before recirculating throughout the body.

Dr. Morris explained that the hole was not life-threatening in the short run, but it did increase Fern's chance of developing irreversible pulmonary hypertension and going into pulmonary arrest.

At only a few millimeters wide, the hole in Fern's heart would be considered a minor nuisance just about anywhere else in life. You would not consider throwing away your favorite pair of jeans if they had a hole this big in the knee. A hole this big in a burrito probably wouldn't even leak salsa. But the hole in my baby's heart was just the right size to be a scapegoat, big enough to carry the blame for why she was so small, so lethargic, so slow to eat. Tiny as it was, it was big enough to be considered a threat to Fern's future health.

"And is there any incentive for waiting until she weighs at least eight pounds before going ahead with the surgery?" I asked.

"No." Dr. Morris answered. "We often see better outcomes in kids who are young and small. The sooner we fix the problem, the sooner she can get on track for growth."

This touched a nerve. Getting Fern to grow remained our primary focus. She was gaining weight at half the rate of her peers, and her twin, Sylvan, was there to remind us every day what "normal" weight gain looked like. The cynic in me wondered whether the hospital just needed to sell another heart surgery that month. Did the need to create revenue influence how urgent Fern's case was? Certainly for us money played a factor.

Once again, I found myself asking, "Okay, where do we go from here?"

Not surprisingly, Dr. Morris had an answer prepared for me. "There is an opening on the surgery schedule 10 days from now."

FOURTEEN

Fiddlehead Gets Her Ticker Fixed

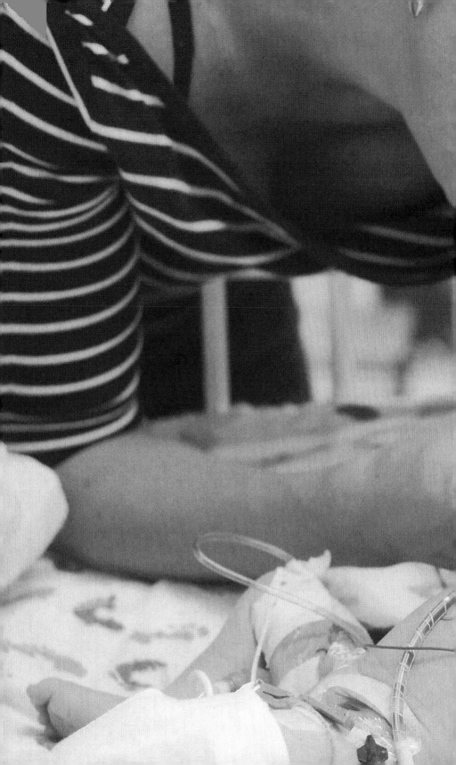

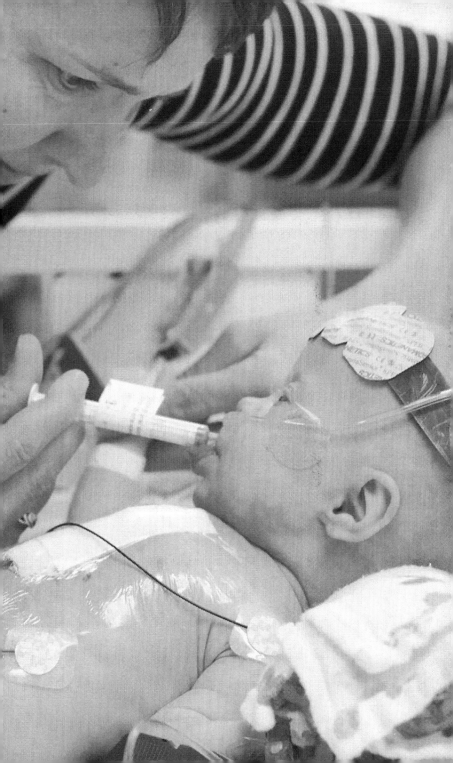

We had ten days to get ready for the surgery. Physically, there wasn't much to do except stay well. No one, especially Fern, was to get sick, otherwise we would have to reschedule the surgery. We canceled all appointments and outings and lived in voluntary quarantine.

Mentally and emotionally? Well, you could have given me a lifetime to prepare and I still would not have been able to imagine the moment when I handed over my 7 pound, 4-month-old baby girl to a team of strangers so they could cut her open and mend a hole in her heart.

From the day Fern was born, we had known that this surgery was very probably in her future. Every time I introduced Fern, I would somehow work the fact that she has Down syndrome and needed heart surgery into the conversation. Sometimes it made sense, like when someone commented on the size difference between Fern and Sylvan. I would almost always answer, "Well, she has Down syndrome and her heart is working extra hard because she has a hole in her heart. She's going to have heart surgery soon to fix that. Then she'll probably start growing faster." Other times, it wasn't always so smooth. Someone might say, "Oh! I love your new sweater!" And I'd say, "Thanks. I bought it because maybe it's going to be chilly in the hospital where my daughter is having heart surgery."

Looking back, this was probably just my way of coping with the unthinkable. I guess I figured if I said it enough, I could actually convince myself that handing your baby over to a team of surgeons was a perfectly normal thing to do. But no matter how many times a doctor does this surgery every week (Fern's surgeon performed the surgery at least three times a week on children and infants) and no matter how great their track record (Fern's surgeon had a 0% mortality rate), it's only ever going to happen to *my* baby once. I educated myself, but I was never really convinced that it was perfectly normal.

I poured over the literature the doctors sent home with us. I studied the diagrams, read the answers to "Frequently Asked Questions," and familiarized myself with the basic time-line from when Fern would be admitted to the hospital until she would be release. There wasn't enough space remaining in my mental hard drive for me to even consider what recovery would look like.

A few days before the surgery, when I still could not get my head around what was about to happen to my baby girl, I thought to call the number on the business card to ask some questions. The woman who answered the phone was friendly and very much wanted to be of assistance. I had a list of 14 questions that the brochures did not answer. I asked, "How long after the surgery will it be until I can see my baby?" And, "After the surgery, will I be allowed to feed my baby breast milk with a bottle I bring in from home?" And, "Will her twin be allowed in the PICU, or will we need to make other arrangements for him?"

The nurse said, "These are all really great questions. I'll try to get some answers for you and call you back."

I was surprised, and a little disappointed. "Oh. You don't know the answers to these questions?"

The nurse said kindly, "No, no one has ever asked them before."

"Really? No one has ever asked when they can see their baby after the surgery? Or how many people can be by her bedside at a time?"

"No. You're the first."

"What's wrong with people? How do they prepare for this kind of thing?"

The nurse laughed. "Well, you have to remember that I deal with the general public and, well, people aren't really all that smart."

True to her word, the nurse had answers for me later that day. But rather than call me back herself, she had a resident surgeon who would be assisting with the surgery call me. He gave me 10 undivided minutes of attention, calmly answering every question on my list, and a few more. If they thought I was a tightly wound, high maintenance pain-in-the-ass, they never let on.

Even with answers to my questions, I still couldn't relax. Sometimes if I can visualize what I'm anxious about, I can release some of my fears and worries. So, the day before Fern's surgery, I put the kids down for a nap in their Ronald McDonald House cribs and then crawled into my own stiff twin bed to walk myself through the impossible.

First, Fern would be prepped for surgery. To construct this imaginary scenario, I relied on what I'd learned from the materials they'd sent home with us. According to a pamphlet, there would be approximately twelve tubes and needles penetrating Fern's body, along with several monitors taped to her head and chest. Needles would be inserted into her arm for the sedation, a catheter would be pushed into her pee hole, and IV fluids would hang from bags on silver hooks near her head. I tried to make it as real as possible for myself by seeing, in my mind's eye, Fern's fuzzy head and mottled skin being jostled and poked by people wearing gloves and masks. I tried to imagine the smell of my baby mingling with the smells of the disinfectants and latex.

The pamphlet explained that Fern's heart would be stopped for the operation and a heart lung machine would pump and oxygenate her blood. One of the tubes coming out of her body would divert her blood to the machine, and another tube entering her body would carry it back.

When your heart stops, doesn't that mean you're dead? Never mind.

In my imagination, the operating room would be cold and surprisingly calm. Fern's team of doctors and nurses (some of the best in the world, naturally) would not blast music or chat idly, like the characters on *Grey's Anatomy* did. They would be focused and efficient. They would work quickly, but not hurriedly.

At some point, a strange skin-like material would be stuck to Fern's chest, marking the site of the incision. Then someone would say, "Dr. Cordon, the patient is ready."

The surgeon would step forward, black-curly hair tucked neatly under a cap and scrubs covered with a clean surgical smock. Holding out a hand that, when we met a few days prior, I deemed steady, if on the small side, Dr. Cordon would say what everyone knows a surgeon says when they are about to begin a surgery.

"Scalpel."

This is the part where I had to work hard to focus my imagination lens. I could see a gloved hand holding a shiny scalpel pointed at the skin-like tape stuck to my baby girl's chest. When the point of the scalpel pierced her skin, Fern's chest would bleed as the prick became a sliver, then widened into a gap.

Someone would have to break her little tiny chest bones. The Sunday before Fern's surgery, I roasted a seven pound chicken and paid special attention to the breast bone as I divided up the chicken for dinner. Later that evening I held Fern and felt her tiny chest bones with my fingers, trying to imagine what it would take to break them open. Would a pair of kitchen scissors do it? A sharp knife?

Fern isn't even 18 inches long, so I have a hard time imagining how they will hold her chest open so the surgeon's assistant can, in her words, "move stuff out of the way." That's how she explained it to me when I asked what a surgeon's assistant does. She told me that she "moves stuff out of the way" so the surgeon can access Fern's heart

Fern is tiny. Her heart is tiny. The hole in her heart is tinier still. In my imagination, the surgeon and his assistant are like giants, with giant hands using giant tools to determine the outcome of the biggest battle there is: my baby's life versus her untimely death.

Now the surgeon, who is going to patch a hole INSIDE of something that is the size of a walnut, cuts open Fern's non-beating heart.

Actually. Cuts. Her. Heart.

This goes against everything my small brain understands about the body. Suddenly, even though I'm only imagining this surgery in my curled position under my bed covers, I feel tense. The heart is an organ. It has a very specific function and it is not designed to be stopped and cut open. And this isn't just any heart. This heart belongs to a little girl, my baby, and we have so much yet to do together.

Wait. Isn't this the incredibly critical part where the surgeon has to be careful not to hit what he called the "electrical circuitry", or else Fern might have to wear a pacemaker the rest of her life? Okay, so in the scene I am making up for myself, the surgeon is very careful not to hit the electrical circuit. Good.

My imaginary surgeon says, "Patch."

I can't remember if he's going to use the synthetic patch or the one made from a pig's gut. I think we told him to use his own discretion, as if it were no big deal we were being consulted on the matter. As if we had bigger decisions to make, like what to have for lunch. I guess there are people with religious objections to having pig parts in their bodies, but when the surgeons are playing god, it seems like a weird time to invoke a no-pork rule.

I can't remember exactly how the surgeon will attach the patch, only he must be very careful not to get too close to the valve, lest the patch be sucked into the valve. It's like a children's book with repeating phrases and a nonsensical ending: There's a tiny heart that has a tiny valve next to a tiny hole that needs a tiny patch, and don't touch the electrical circuit!

As I lay in my bed, trying to make this impossible thing real for myself, my imaginary surgeon steps back and says, "Let's close her up."

I try to recall the brochure for details on how Fern's heart will be restarted, how Fern's blood will be returned to her body, and how her chest bones will be reconnected. But I am tired and I find I must surrender the need to understand even the most basic aspects of the surgery. I'm frustrated because I don't even know enough to ask the right questions. All I can do is trust that the doctors are giving me the best advice they possibly can. That the economic incentive for them to perform this surgery on my daughter is less persuasive than the actual benefit of the surgery.

The fate of my daughter was out of my hands and, quite literally, in the hands of strangers who, I prayed, would get a good night's rest and eat a balanced breakfast before they showed up to work on the day of my child's surgery. I planned to do the same. Although it might not be as esteemed or demanding as a surgeon's, tomorrow my job, as a mother, was going to be every bit as important.

FIFTEEN

Falling for Fern

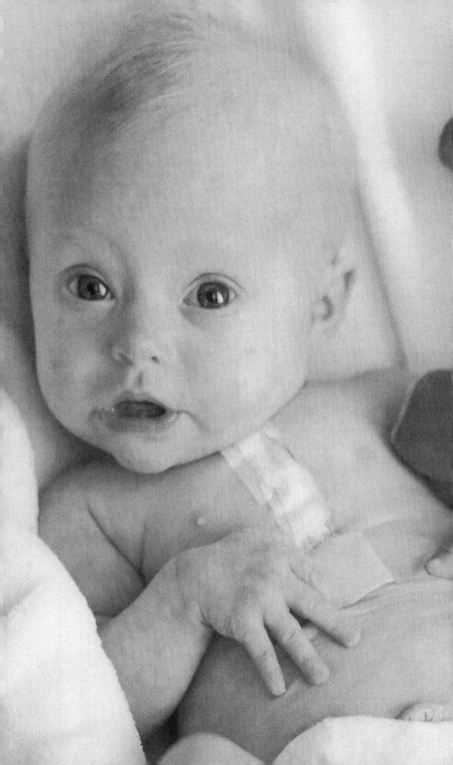

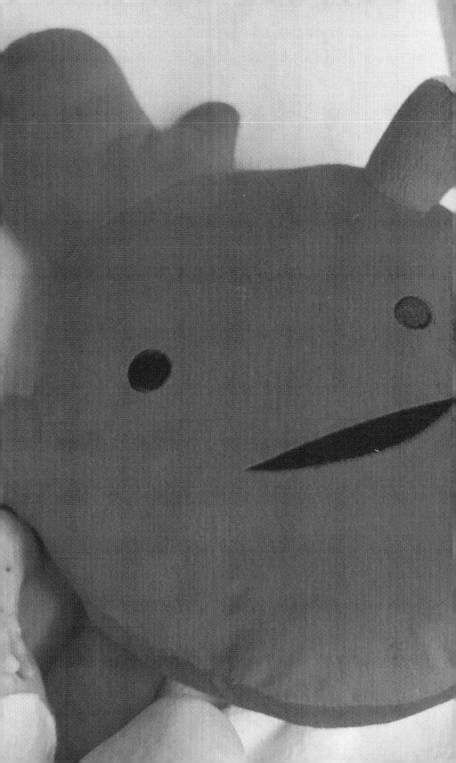

It takes me a long time to fall in love with my babies. This was something I was very glad to know about myself when I found out that one of my twins had Down syndrome. Otherwise, I might have blamed Fern's diagnosis for why I did not feel connected to her in the early months, further complicating my relationship with her.

Insofar as motherly instincts go, I had the baseline mommy stuff covered from the start. From the moment I met each of my three children, I happily cared for them, felt fiercely protective of them and found myself fascinated by their tiny existence. In the days after our first son, Cypress, was born, my husband and I spent hours staring at him in disbelief. We had a baby! He was born, he was perfect, and he was ours to keep! And yet, as enamored as I was with this new being, we were, after all, only just meeting for the first time. We needed time to get to know one another and several months passed before my heart swelled with the pressure of excruciatingly boundless love I now understand to be a mother's love.

When I first met Fern, the only thing I wanted was for her to not have Down syndrome. Once I accepted that this was not going to happen, the focus of my desire shifted to wanting to love my daughter as unconditionally as I loved my boys. I wanted to feel for her the kind of love that brings a mother to her knees, helpless with the knowledge that no matter what we do to protect them, our children are at the mercy of a world that can be cruel and unfair. It would not be enough for me to have pleasant "warm" feelings for Fern or to simply "accept" her condition and her presence in my life. I needed to feel that, without her, my life would be incomplete, robbed of an element as crucial to my existence as oxygen.

As they say, "love is a verb." I did my best to just show up and be Mom. But Fern and I bore no resemblance to the Madonna and her chubby, rosy cheeked child, the touchstone image of what motherhood is "supposed" to look like. When I passed the mirror on the way to the shower with Fern's naked body draped across my shoulder, I had to avert my eyes because she was just so odd looking. Where my other babies had cute little padded butts and beautiful radiant skin, Fern was skeletal and mottled. My naked body wasn't any easier to look at. My breasts were swollen to abnormally large orbs and there were grotesque slabs of extra skin lying just above my fresh and irritated cesarean scar.

Part of playing the role of "mother" meant coming up with new and creative ways for feeling guilt. I felt guilty for all the time Cypress was spending watching *Bob the Builder* while I nursed and pumped for the twins. I felt guilty for being able to nurse Sylvan but not Fern. I felt guilty when I held one baby and not the other, then felt the same thing in reverse when I switched them around. Between sleep deprivation and the constant demands of three children under the age of two, there wasn't much of me left to go around. And I felt pretty guilty about that too. But most of all, I felt guilty that my feelings for Sylvan were growing strong and undeniable. I found his blue eyes irresistible and his chubby cheeks were easy targets for my kisses. I was feeling pretty guilty about how easily I was falling in love with Sylvan when I was still unsure of what I was feeling for Fern.

In his book *Far from the Tree,* Andrew Solomon points out that one of the great ironies of parenthood is as adults we pride ourselves on being different from our own parents, and yet we are pained when our children are different from ourselves. Fern didn't look like any of us, and she didn't act like any other baby. The usual exchanges that happen between mama and baby that reinforce the bond weren't happening. Sylvan was cooing and reaching for my face when he nursed and responding to my smiles. Fern lacked the gross motor coordination to reach for anything intentionally, and she only looked at me with surprise when I tried to make her smile. We were mother and daughter, but I wasn't certain of the strength of our bond.

Which is why, on the night before Fern's heart surgery, I was surprised to find myself curled up in a heap on the bathroom floor of our room at the Ronald McDonald House, crying. I knew I was scared for Fern and, if I'm honest, scared for myself as well. I worried that the statistics might betray us, yet again, and that we might be the one in 100,000 who has complications from the surgery. I worried that I would be reclassified from "Mother of a child with special needs" to "Bereaved Mother."

But as my tears subsided and I regained my breath, I suddenly understood why I felt so vulnerable and scared. I wasn't just nervous for my baby, this tiny creature I was only just getting to know. I was in love with this child! I was absolutely, positively, undeniably in love with Fern. As she lay in the borrowed RMH crib, sound asleep and oblivious to my melt-down in the bathroom, I was coming to know with absolute certainty that I could, and did, love Fern as much as my other children. Moreover, I didn't love her "in spite of" her having Down syndrome, or because of it. I loved her because she was my daughter, and she was mine to love.

Early the next morning, we walked Fern over to the hospital to check-in for the surgery. Everything went smoothly. Even though she hadn't had anything to eat for several hours, Fern was sweet and mellow. She looked absolutely adorable in her apricot colored mini-hospital gown and I added "apricot" to "her" list of colors. We were guided from check-in to pre-op and finally into a staging area where everyone having surgery that day, some 45 people of various ages, lay in four long rows of hospital beds queued up as if in an assembly line waiting to be repaired by surgeons.

Sylvan was with us throughout this all. This is Sylvan's fate as an exclusively breastfed baby. He and I went everywhere together, and so he was there when the doctors came for Fern. Will was holding Sylvan, and I stood with Fern to greet the team. They were all wearing the same green colored scrubs and hair nets. Only one of them was a woman, and it was she who reached for Fern. I gave Fern one last smooch, then put her into the woman's gloved hands. And then, like a flock of birds, the whole team turned in unison and walked away. As they passed through the double doors, I heard Fern's little cry go up and I lost it just a little bit. Will wisely distracted me by handing over Sylvan and I got myself together enough to walk out of the staging area. As we picked up speed, I was able to come back to myself. Now, all there was to do was wait.

Will and I took Sylvan down to the café for some break-fast, then we met up with Midwife Lucy, who had offered to be helpful in any way possible on the day of Fern's surgery. Midwife Lucy held Sylvan and we passed the time with pleas-ant conversation during which I learned all kinds of important things only a midwife can tell you. Did you know that some Amish women wear Victoria Secret underwear?

Of all the things I appreciated about the team at Clarkes-ville, what I appreciated most was their commitment to good communication. The first 12 hours of Fern's life in the NICU aside, we feel the communication with Fern's care providers has been remarkable. The day of her surgery was no exception. There was a nurse designated to call us with updates through-out the day. She called us every hour as they prepped Fern for surgery, then she called us to say that they were ready to make the incision, and then she called after the surgery itself (which didn't actually take very long!), and finally she called to tell us that Fern was off the heart lung machine and ready to be transferred to the PICU. This was our chance to see her briefly.

We were sitting in the waiting area designated for the PICU which, I soon understood, was situated between the OR and the PICU. So when Fern's surgery was finished, they ac-tually wheeled her hospital bed past the waiting area on their way to the PICU. They stopped briefly so we could see her. I remember feeling very uncertain of how I could interact with her, so I opted to hold back and stand in the doorway. The doctor encouraged me to move forward a little and say hello. Although she was clearly still under some sedation, Fern locked eyes with me. You might think that after her ordeal a four-month-old baby would have looked scared, or confused, or even disoriented. But not Fern. Fern's look penetrated me.

Her eyes bore accusingly into me and clearly conveyed what she was thinking: "What. The hell. Just happened?"

The surgeon and his team continued on to the PICU with Fern, then the good looking Ethiopian doctor came back to debrief us on how the surgery went. He mentioned that they had to give Fern a pint of blood. I asked, "Is that because she lost a lot of blood, or because you had to prime the pump for the heart lung machine so to speak?" He raised his eyebrows and said, "It was to prime the pump, as you say. Are you a nurse?" I said, "No. I read the brochure you sent home with me." He laughed, "Oh, I don't think everyone reads that."

He left promising it would only be another 30 minutes or so before we could see Fern. In reality, it was another two hours of waiting until someone finally came to get us. Later in the week, I was sitting beside Fern's bed when they rolled in a small boy who had just had the same heart surgery. He was maybe two years old and I heard everything that went into getting that child to settle. Other than to cry for "mama," he wasn't old enough to talk. His low, baneful moans were punctuated by piercing, terrified cries, and my eyes welled with tears for him. As tough as it was to get him settled, it was only 35 minutes from the time he was wheeled into recovery until they let in his mother, who had PINK hair and looked kind of ridiculous as a result, making me thankful for the second time in 10 days that I had not acted on my impulse to dye my hair pink for my fortieth birthday.

I will never know what happened during those 2 hours as they tried to "settle" Fern, but just as I was starting to think something must have gone really wrong, her cardiologist came to the waiting room. He greeted us each with a handshake and a warm smile. He explained that Fern was settled and he had

had the chance to do his complete post-operative exam. He smiled and assured us, "There are not enough words to describe how well Fern is doing."

.   .   .

I'm not exactly sure how parents of kids with special needs survived before Facebook. Of the dozens of new supportive friends I've made since having a child with special needs, a few I've never even met face-to-face have played critical roles. One of them is Jana, who offered to show me some photos taken just after her daughter, Mary, had the exact same surgery as Fern.

The brochure we were given had a diagram of a baby prepped for this surgery, with each of the tubes and wires coming out the baby neatly labeled for my study. Now that I had photos of an actual child who had been through the surgery, I could see that the brochure failed to capture the swelling around the eyes, blood leaking from beneath bandages and dry cracked lips. The brochure did not show that the tube leaving from her abdominal cavity drained blood and fluid into a bag tied to the side of the bed, where I would accidentally kick it when I uncrossed my legs while sitting bedside. The baby in the diagram did not have any private parts, so it was up to me to imagine where the tube labeled "catheter" entered the body. The photos of Mary were raw and left little to the imagination. They were hard to look at, but I studied them in hopes that I would not be as shocked when I first saw Fern post-operative.

When they were finally ready for us, we left Sylvan in the care of Midwife Lucy and we followed the nurse to the PICU. There was our baby, vulnerably naked but for all the bandages, tubes, and monitors stuck to her. I was stunned, but I was prepared. As promised, there were twelve tubes entering and exiting Fern's body, along with a pulse-ox taped to her toe, some kind of electronic reader taped to her head, and several bonus echo pads taped to her head and body. Fern looked terrible, but she looked as I expected she would. And there was some comfort in knowing that Mary had once looked just like this and was now a healthy and happy child. Fern would pull through too.

As I stood over my baby, unable to pick her up, unable to soothe her with anything other than a small syringe of sweet water, I prayed that we had made the right decision to go ahead with the surgery, that this would be the turning point we needed for Fern. To put her through the pain and suffering without the promised payoff would be unjust.

We spent the rest of the afternoon with Fern, taking turns to be with her while she slept, offering what little comfort we could when she woke. But we took the nurses advice when she suggested both Fern and her parents could use some rest and quiet time. We said goodbye to Midwife Lucy and headed back to the RMH, Sylvan in tow.

That night, Fern's empty crib made me feel sad. I missed her. I hated that she was alone in the PICU. When she moved to the pediatrics floor, we would be able to sleep in the room with her. But for now, she was there alone except for the nurses who prodded and monitored her.

After Sylvan's 4 A.M. feeding, I laid in my bed for a few minutes thinking about Fern and considered my options. In those days, sleep was always an allure, as it seemed there was never enough to go around. The temptation to fall back asleep for a couple of hours until Sylvan was up for the day competed with my desire to sneak out and go see Fern. I got up.

As quietly as possible, I dressed with whatever I could find in the dark which, sadly, did not include a bra. I put on a baseball cap and slid into my sneakers. Then I whispered in Will's ear that I was headed for the PICU and that he should bring Sylvan over whenever they were ready for the day. I slipped out of our room, grabbed one of the energy bars I'd made for this trip, and went out into the cold, dark autumn morning. I walked quickly, getting to the PICU in about the time it took for me to eat the energy bar and an apple. It was 4:15 am and the nurse was surprised to see me, but she quickly debriefed me on what happened overnight.

Fern was sleeping, naked but for the long bandage running down her chest and a light blanket draped over her legs. I grabbed a magazine from the waiting area and sat down in a chair next to her bed. Then I waited. I wanted to make sure I was there when she woke up the next time, and as many times as possible after that. After about an hour, she stirred. I stood over her, stroking her downy head, and she looked at me with confused, sleepy eyes.

"Hey baby girl. You did great. You did so great. Mama loves you so much." I cried for the truth of it. I loved her so much, and I knew that love was only growing more intense by the day.

That night, instead of pajamas, I slept in a nursing bra, a long sleeve shirt and clean yoga pants. I lined up my shoes and socks by the door, where I also had a snack bag and water bottle ready to grab. I wanted to go to Fern again the next morning, and every morning after that. No longer just her manager, I was magnetized to her. More than ever, I was embracing my role as mother to my baby girl who had Down syndrome, but who no longer had a problem with her heart. For whom my love was all the sweeter because it did not come easily.

When I was still pregnant and we were thinking of names for the twins, I really wanted to call the girl, Baby B, Fern Aubrey. In my mind, Fern was non-negotiable and I loved that Aubrey meant something like "elf leader." But Will wasn't convinced. We figured we'd be inspired after the twins were born, but then we were too distracted by Fern's diagnosis for anything like inspiration to take hold. Two days after they were born, the hospital staff insisted we get serious about naming the babies. So, we took out the list of names we'd been batting around. With some sadness, I realized that Fern did look like a little elf, but not in a way that I wanted to celebrate. Instead, we decided to go with what, prenatally, seemed ridiculous but now felt almost imperative. During one of our prenatal name-games, Will had suggested we give Fern the middle name "Maya" which means "love" in Nepalese. I didn't really like the name, and I felt like giving a child a name that meant "love" was just too cheesy, the kind of feel-good-thing Will was always dragging me into. But once we had Fern's diagnosis it seemed like she could use all the love she could get. Her big brother Cypress's middle name, Pax, means peace, so that only left Happiness, which is how Sylvan ended up with the middle name Felix.

It's no small irony that the child I struggled to love ended up teaching me the most about love. Fern Maya showed me that the rules I was taught about love were meant to be broken. Having Fern gave me singular focus, and I let go of the fools who could never give me the love I needed and I harnessed all that freed up energy to focus on the people who appreciate, and reciprocate, my kind of love. Fern Maya has shown me that I greatly underestimated my capacity and the capacity of others to love and that, given the opportunity, people clamor to love the unlovable. Love is not just a pie for which we must all fight over a single slice, rather it is limitless and endlessly replenishing its stores.

You might say that we both had our hearts fixed that week. Fern, in her innocence and youth, needed the help of a surgeon to mend the hole in her heart and I, middle-aged and hardened, needed the help of a 7-pound giant. My daughter had open-heart surgery, but as we sat together in the pediatric intensive care unit, rocking and healing together, it was really me whose heart was opened.

SIXTEEN

The Letter I was too Chicken Shit

to Send to My Friend

Dear Marcy,

It was nice to run into you the other day. Funny how we keep bumping into each other!

I'm writing to follow up on the conversation we had while standing in the produce section. I felt like it ended on a weird note and I just wanted to make sure everything is okay between us.

As you probably recall, we were talking about my baby girl's recent heart surgery. I know you meant well when you said, "God doesn't give you any more than you can handle." And we both had a good chuckle when I said, "Yes he does. That's why I'm on antidepressants."

But Marcy, I have to be honest with you: I was hoping you'd be a better listener. We've been friends for years and you know that it was quite a shock for me to learn that Fern had Down syndrome. Now she is recovering from open heart surgery and flu season is here. I was trying to share with you how worried I am for her. This is all very scary stuff and I guess I thought you might be a source of comfort. But instead of lending a listening ear, it felt like you shrugged off my feelings by saying, "God doesn't give you any more than you can handle."

And then, well, I guess things got really weird when I said, "Actually, I no longer believe in God."

Your eyes widened and your face turned bright red. You tried to hide your surprise but in the moment it took for you to recover, I read your thoughts.

You think I'm mad at God for giving me a kid who has Down syndrome and you think I'm angry with God because Fern needed heart surgery. You think I'm going to regret turning my back on God during a time when I might need him most. And, if I'm not mistaken, you're also a little worried that you might somehow be on the hook for saving my soul, lest I end up condemned to hell for being a non-believer.

In some ways, you're right. When I first learned that Fern had Down syndrome, I was very mad at God. I said things like, "Fuck you God, for thinking I can do this." And, "Screw you for choosing me." But those feelings quickly passed. My relationship with God had been on the rocks long before Fern came along, and her diagnosis only brought everything into focus for me. When I turned to God as a source of comfort during some of the hardest months of my life, God wasn't there. In fact, there wasn't even a hole where God used to be. So, you see, Marcy, I'm not mad at God. I can't be mad at something that isn't there.

As for my soul, well, I take full responsibility. For years I credited a higher power for giving me the clarity and strength I needed to rise out of a life populated by drunks and liars. I am so thankful for my present life where I am surrounded by friends who are healthy, whole and generally happy. It seemed the more connected I felt to God, the happier I was. The more content I was with my life, the more connected I felt to God. No one is more surprised than me to learn that giving up God does not mean giving up my sense of wonder, or my wish to live from a place of gratitude, or my desire to truly care for others. I can feel connected and happy without channeling those feeling through God. Or maybe I should clarify and say I DO feel connected and happy, and I do not need a God to validate that for me.

Marcy, you are a good person and I know you mean well, but I want to encourage you to dig a little deeper the next time you are listening to a friend who is hurting, whether they are a Christian or not. Saying things like, "God has a plan," and "God singled you out to be Fern's mother" and, "She's a special miracle sent from heaven," almost feels like you're saying, "Good thing God is going to be there for you, because I certainly won't be!" What people really need when they are experiencing trauma is some assurance that their earthly friends and family will be there to help them through it. You might trying saying something like, "Oh, man. This sounds like a really hard time. What can I do to be helpful?"

Right now, cynicism and religion are much the same to me. I don't want to give up my convictions about God and take up instead a conviction that there is no God. I'm not trying to convince anyone of anything. I probably shouldn't have said anything at the grocery store. I could have just smiled and nodded like I have a hundred times before when people have said, "God doesn't give you any more than you can handle." I think, though, because we're friends, I just wanted you to know just how empty those words are to me.

Very truly,
Heather

SEVENTEEN

Fern's Formula

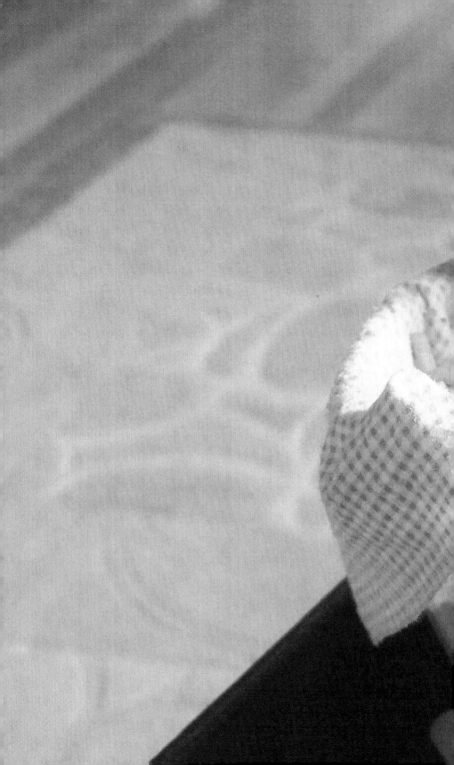

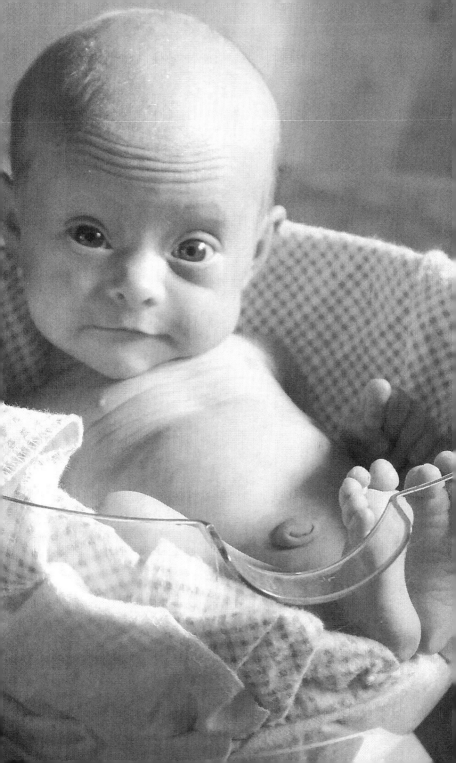

The hope was that after the hole in Fern's heart was mended, she would begin to put on weight at the same rate as her peers. But after several months of healing and concentrated feeding, Fern was still small. Which is why I requested an appointment with a pediatric nutritionist.

Fern lay on the examination table undressed, but for her diaper, giggling in response to the bicycle motions I made with her legs. She had just turned eight-months-old and we were enjoying a rare mommy-and-me moment, without either of her brothers present. This appointment was an important one and I asked Will to watch the boys so I could concentrate on my conversation with the doctor. However, when I practiced what I was going to say to Fern's pediatric nutritionist in my head, I never imagined she would be 10 years younger than me. So when the barely-thirty-something woman walked into the room, I found myself recalculating my strategy.

The young doctor greeted us warmly. "Hello, I'm Dr. Gastro. This must be Fern."

"Yes," I answered. "You're young."

I can't help myself. It's as though I have no filter between my head and my mouth.

Dr. Gastro laughed. "People often think I'm younger than I actually am."

Dr. Gastro gave Fern a big smile and I left it at that. It dawned on me that being older than my daughter Fern's doctor might give me a psychological advantage. If nothing else, it gave me a sense of confidence that I sorely needed at the moment. Dr. Gastro had access to information I wanted, but getting at it would mean disclosing a secret I had been working hard to keep.

Dr. Gastro took a look at the purplish scar on Fern's chest. "How is Fern doing since she had heart surgery?"

"Well, it seems like she's doing great. At least, she's off all the heart medications and it appears the surgery was a success. The only thing now is that she is still growing kind of slowly."

Dr. Gastro pulled up Fern's medical chart on the computer. "Yes," she said. "While she's gaining steadily, she's still in the bottom 20th percentile for weight and also the bottom fifth percentile for height."

I nodded and said, "And that's the growth chart for premature babies you're looking at. She's not even on the chart for typically developing babies."

Fern was born 3lbs 14oz and just one month premature, but her growth rate lagged behind premies with even lower birth weights. For months, Fern's stats didn't register on the charts her peers were using either, the one for kids who have Down syndrome. And, although it didn't exist, I suspected she would not have even made much of a showing on a growth chart dedicated to premature babies with Down syndrome born with a heart defect and a thyroid disorder who were also a twin. Fern was small. Even among small people.

Dr. Gastro swiveled in her chair to face me. She had a pleasant, open face framed by smooth dark hair. "And so, you are here today to see if there is a nutritional reason for this slow growth?"

"Yes," I answered, reminding myself that just because my hair was curly and unruly it did not mean I was a flake.

Dr. Gastro turned her attention back to Fern, who was very slowly passing a fat stick from one hand to another.

At eight-months-old, Fern had not yet developed the trunk muscles needed to sit unassisted, and even when I held her upright, she still had the tendency to slouch to one side or the other. Fern's twin, Sylvan, could sit up unassisted and I never even noticed when he started passing objects from one hand to another. It is the kind of milestone you don't even realize is a milestone until your kid isn't doing it. After months of watching Fern's every move for signs of this emerging coordination, I had almost fainted when just a couple of weeks prior, propped up in her Bumbo chair, she transferred my make-up brush from her right hand to her left.

"She looks wonderfully healthy to me. Her color is good. She has fat in all the right places." Fern's watchful blue-gray eyes stayed trained on Dr. Gastro as she did her examination. "Her hair is shiny. Her eyes are bright. Her attention is good, reaction time is normal for a baby with Down syndrome. Other than being small, she looks really healthy to me."

"That's good to hear," I said. I love being reassured by Fern's doctors that what I believe is true actually is true. "I think she finally looks healthy too."

Fern's coloring was typical of kids with Down syndrome, and noticeably different from everyone else's in our family. She was born a distressing jaundiced yellow-green, and once that cleared up she turned an almost translucent pale pink with prominent mottling lines. But at eight months old, the mottling had subsided and she was finally a beautiful, healthy peachy color.

Dr. Gastro listened to Fern's heart and looked into Fern's impossibly small ear canals. Fern squirmed in her baby blue cloth diaper and reached for the stethoscope with tiny *dimpled* hands. "Are you feeding her any solids yet?"

"Yes, she loves sweet potatoes and pears especially."

Dr. Gastro palpated Fern's belly and took a peek inside her diaper. "And is she digesting food okay? Pooping regularly? Not too gassy or fussy after eating?"

"Mostly. We've made a few adjustments here and there. But mostly she's tolerating solids really well. She rarely gags and she's not too picky. She even swallows most of what we put in her mouth!"

No small feat for a baby with Down syndrome. Swallowing requires a certain mastery of the tongue that does not come easily to babies with Down syndrome, or typically developing babies for that matter. We all have to *learn* to eat.

Dr. Gastro finished her exam of Fern and returned to her computer to make some notes. "Are you still breastfeeding Fern?"

"Fern never actually breastfed," I answered as I re-dressed Fern in a cozy baby sweat suit. "I was pumping for her, so she was fed breast milk exclusively until she was six-months-old. From a bottle."

Dr. Gastro continued typing as we talked. "And now you are feeding her formula?"

"Yes."

Dr. Gastro pulled up another page in Fern's medical record. "What brand are you using?"

I knew this question was coming. They ask it every time, and my plan was to use it as segue to why I had requested this appointment. "Well, that's what I want to talk to you about."

The keys on the keyboard went tap tap tap. "What can I help you with?"

I picked up Fern and sat her on my lap. Up until now, anytime a doctor asked me what brand of formula I was feeding Fern, I gave a vague answer. "Oh, you know. It changes. We're experimenting to see what works best." And while this was not a blatant lie, it was not the whole truth.

This time, I needed to tell the whole truth. "I want to tell you something completely off the record, "I said. "I don't want you to record it on Fern's medical chart. This cannot get back to Fern's primary care doctor and I don't want her cardiologist catching wind of it either. Can you do that for me?"

Dr. Gastro swiveled in her chair to face me. She cocked her head to the side while she thought for a moment. "Well, I can't promise that. If I learn of something that concerns me or is jeopardizing the health of your child, I have an obligation to report it."

"Fair enough. Hopefully we can agree that this is not that a big of a deal," I said. "The thing is…we are making Fern's formula from scratch."

Dr. Gastro nodded. "Okay. I have heard of mothers doing this."

Relieved that Dr. Gastro was open to the discussion, I said, "But you have not worked with anyone who makes their child's formula before?"

"No, this is a first."

I was not sure whether this was good news or bad news. It was great that Dr. Gastro didn't appear to have any preconceived notions about what it meant to make your child's formula. But not very helpful if it turned out I needed to make some modifications to Fern's formula.

I stroked Fern's downy blonde hair. It had been a long eight months. When I first learned Fern had Down syndrome, my world was flipped upside down. How did I not know she was going to be born with Down syndrome? I questioned everything about my prenatal care, which fed a deep mistrust of doctors even as my newborn daughter was in the NICU, dependent on doctors for everything. Now, just when I was starting to regain confidence in the decisions I was making for Fern, nagging doubt sprang from behind the bushes and accused me of undernourishing my child. Even if it meant becoming a target of this doctor's ridicule, I was going to put all my cards on the table in hopes of getting some reassurance I was on the right track.

"Okay, well, the reason I wanted to meet with you today is to make sure that Fern's formula is nutritionally sound. That it's not some problem with the formula that's causing her to grow so slowly."

"Well, I can almost guarantee just by looking at her that she does not have a nutritional deficiency. This is not a child who is mal-fed. But I'd be glad to run a nutritional analysis on the formula." Dr. Gastro grabbed a pen and a notepad. "I'll just need specifics on what you are putting in the formula. I assume it starts with milk?"

"Yes. But this is the part that I don't want you to put on her permanent record." Dr. Gastro tilted her head to one side again, waiting for me to go on. "We use raw milk."

Dr. Gastro smiled at me, finally understanding why I was acting so weird. "I see. And you think that as a doctor I would have a problem with that?"

"Yes," I said. And then hurriedly added, "I want to be clear that I'm not here asking for your opinion on whether raw milk is safe. I just want to know if the formula I'm making is meeting my baby's nutritional needs."

About year prior, my husband took our oldest child to the doctor for a routine check-up and mentioned that Cypress had weaned and was drinking raw milk instead. After my husband left the doctor's office, the doctor called me at home to tell me that she strongly opposed raw milk and that she felt I was irresponsible for letting Cypress drink it. After a doctor calls you 'irresponsible,' it's hard not to feel defensive.

Drinking raw milk is a risk. I knew this. Raw milk can contain harmful pathogens that can lead to serious illness, a lifetime of health complications or even death. The populations most likely to be most severely affected are the very young and the very old. A baby who gets sick from drinking raw milk can suffer from kidney failure, stroke, and permanent bowel damage. A perfectly healthy child can be paralyzed for life if they are infected by the "bad" bacteria. They may even die. I did not question the legitimacy of these claims. And still, I chose to feed Fern raw milk.

Dr. Gastro shrugged. "I don't have a problem with you feeding Fern raw milk."

Relief and disbelief caught me off guard. "You don't?"

"No. I grew up on a dairy farm. I'm not worried about you feeding your daughter raw milk. I assume you feel confident you getting it from a clean source?"

As quick as commercially pasteurized milk turns from "smells okay" to "freakishly spoiled," Dr. Gastro went from being my assumed opponent to being my ally. "Yes! We have a great source!" I put Fern up on my shoulder and she pulled at my curls while I gushed excitedly about our local farmer who has small children who drink the milk too.

Dr. Gastro nodded. "There are a lot of great family farms around here. So, can you tell me the recipe for the formula you are making?"

I dug in Fern's diaper bag, pulled out a piece of paper and handed it to the doctor. "The current recipe I am using has over 15 ingredients, so I typed it up for you. That's the ingredients, the measurements and even the brand names of vitamins so you can be precise in your calculations."

Dr. Gastro looked at the long list. "I'll need some time to run the numbers, but I'll call you with the results by Friday."

"That would be great," I said as I bent to put Fern in her stroller and gave the new fat rolls on her thighs a squeeze.

As I was packing up the diaper bag, Dr. Gastro said, "I know Fern's doctor pretty well. I have worked with her in the PICU. She wouldn't be upset to hear you're feeding Fern raw milk. In fact, she'll tell you that it's been a long time since a baby died from drinking raw milk. She's been caring for kids for a long time and she's not influenced by hype and fear like young doctors can be."

Funny, coming from you.

"And even if you don't personally have a problem with it, you don't have some kind of professional responsibility to try to get me to change my ways?" The Center for Disease Control and the Federal Department of Agriculture both had clear statements against the consumption of raw milk.

"No. It's not like you are doing anything that is likely to harm your child."

I fastened the straps on Fern's stroller. "Okay, I'm relieved to hear that. Thank you."

That went better than I expected.

.   .   .

Feeding Fern commercial formula would have been the path of least resistance. We could have even received it free from WIC. Scoop of powder, add water, avoid feeling defensive around the Modern Medical Machine. Done.

But we never seriously considered feeding Fern a commercially produced formula. Every now and then I would start to fret that maybe my homemade formula was the reason why Fern wasn't growing, and I would find myself standing in the formula aisle reading labels for lists of ingredients that started with something other than "corn solids." It seemed like the more "digestible" a formula claimed to be, the less actual food it contained. I could never convince myself that buying a reconstituted product designed by scientists and produced by factories sourcing the cheapest possible inputs would be better for my daughter than something I made at home, from real food.

Of course, the ideal food for Fern would have been breast milk. When it became clear that Fern was never going to latch properly, I made a commitment to pump breast milk for her for at least six months. But pumping did not come easily for me. It was as if my body was never fully convinced it needed to make enough milk for two babies. I had a brand new breast pump with the sucking action of a Dyson vacuum cleaner, but my body did not respond to the mechanical stimulation. Instead, Sylvan had to be nursing one breast in order for me to pump the other breast for Fern. My supply was barely adequate and I was often pumping the very bottle that Fern was hungry for. I tried everything to increase my production, from taking every galactogogue under the sun to drinking over two gallons of water a day, from working with lactation consultants to using breast massage and visualizations to encourage let down. I was spending as much as two hours a day at the pump, occasionally in the back of my minivan if an outing overlapped a feeding, because the one thing you hear over and over again is that your body will respond to the demands you place on it. Demand more milk and your body will make more milk. Bullshit.

My nipples were sore, my supply was low and other than working my way through six seasons of Mad Men on the iPad, I enjoyed nothing about the time I spent pumping. It was messy, time consuming, frustrating and painful.

So, on her six-month birthday, I weighed the benefits of feeding Fern breast milk against the cost of continuing the battle with my supply. If we weren't going to have that breast-feeding bond, which I simultaneously mourned as a loss and resented for being a source of mommy-guilt, shouldn't I at least give her the most perfect nutrition? Probably. But motherhood is like soil that you have lovingly prepared as a place for your ideologies to thrive but that is often overtaken with the weeds of compromise. My New Year's reality was that I was an unhappy, tired mommy chasing after a barely two-year-old and two six-month-olds. I needed relief and I decided to free myself from the bonds of pumping. Effective immediately.

Feeding Fern homemade formula was an unintentional act of protest. It's not that I was looking for a fight. I wasn't trying to make a statement by making my baby's formula from scratch. In fact, I told almost no one what I was doing for fear I would be forced to defend my parenting decision, something I loathe doing. I was only looking for something I felt comfortable feeding my six-month-old baby. I was trying to listen to my intuition and think for myself. As my friend said to me, in an age when there is tension between the die-hard breastfeeders and mothers who, whether they choose to or have to, feed their babies commercially produced formula, there's something about *making* formula for your baby with healthy, whole food that is "sadly radical."

That Fern's formula was based on raw milk only made the act seem more subversive. But after taking a look at my options for what kind of milk to use in the formula, including a source for local pasteurized milk that came in glass bottles, I decided to feed Fern raw milk from a farm where the cows grazed on grass and the farmer shook my hand.

My homemade formula was inspired by the recipe developed by the sometimes looney, sometimes wise, almost always controversial people at The Weston A. Price Foundation. They are best known for their role in polarizing the debate over the dangers versus the health benefits of drinking raw milk. Many of their claims are backed by science, many are not. A number of their claims are based on anecdotal evidence provided by raw milk enthusiasts, and they can be a very passionate group of people. To hear them tell it, drinking raw milk is like drinking from the fountain of youth. It cures what ails you, repopulates the bacteria in your gut, and, in doing so, adds years to your life. Proponents claim that unpasteurized milk is nutritionally superior to pasteurized milk and much easier to digest. Many people who are lactose intolerant say that they can digest unpasteurized milk. Some proponents believe that raw milk is like a perfect ecosystem and that, left alone, the good bacteria will win out over the bad bacteria and the chances of someone getting sick from raw milk are very low.

Opponents, on the other hand, assert that raw milk is at the root of all things evil and any claims of health benefits are made only by charlatans and snake oil salesmen. Opponents insist there are not *significant* nutritional benefits to drinking raw milk, and that there are other ways to get good bacteria in your gut. Both the CDC and FDA insist there is no evidence suggesting raw milk is easier to digest than pasteurized milk. And both organizations address the myth that raw milk can't make you sick because it is a perfect ecosystem: it can and has made people very ill.

As with most polarized debates, things aren't actually so black and white. As I tried to sort the issue out for myself, I wanted to know where were the rational people speaking about the risks of raw milk without using fear tactics? And where were the proponents who touted the benefits of raw milk without promising the holy land? In trying to navigate where I wanted to be on the continuum of Earth Mama versus Science Mama, I realized that I wanted to be an Earthy Science Mama. Or maybe it was a Scientific Earth Mama? However you put it, I wanted to see the science that either supported or clearly contradicted the natural, instinctive earth mama decisions that felt most important to me. Instead, I felt the familiar tension that rises whenever I am about to challenge conventional wisdom. I hate it when my mommy intuition collides with fear-based science.

In the end, like a lot of parenting decisions, choosing to feed Fern raw milk was a decision as emotional as it was rational. As someone who is lactose intolerant, my personal experience played out that raw milk was, indeed, much more digestible than pasteurized milk. Drink pasteurized milk, have farts. Drink raw milk, husband will still sleep in the same room with you. Plus, raw milk just tastes better.

I finally came to realize that I was perfectly comfortable with what my research led me to believe was only a mildly elevated and way overblown risk of serving my children raw milk. It was the judgment of others that made me uncomfortable. In the defense I had prepared for Fern's pediatric nutritionist, I planned to sucker punch helicopter parenting and ask her, "Is the world we are trying to protect our children from really all that dangerous, or have we become too afraid of litigation and the judgment of others to think for ourselves?"

Before I fed Fern anything, I wanted to be sure the formula was nutritionally sound and not just something that looked good on paper to a subversive group of pro-food anti-government farm activists (among whom I proudly count myself). I entered the recipe I was using into an online calculator and learned that my homemade recipe contained about the same number of calories per serving as breast milk. The profiles for protein, fat, carbohydrates and vitamins were also similar. Although I had no way of comparing more complex things like amino acids and trace minerals, and though the formula would never contain any of the great antibodies that shore up the immune system of a nursing baby, the recipe seemed sound.

We had a two day supply of breast milk in the freezer to use up before I introduced the new formula to Fern. Over those two days, I had private conversations with Fern about why mommy was no longer going to pump breast milk for her. In the journal I keep for the babies, I wrote to Fern explaining my decision and how sometimes the best way to show a person you love them is to take care of yourself first. On the third day, when we ran out of what little surplus of breast milk I had stored in the freezer, I offered Fern her first bottle of homemade formula. And she loved it.

Personally, it was nothing I wanted to drink on a daily basis, but Fern seemed to find the formula tasty. There were a few kinks to work out and I was constantly fiddling with the recipe. When Fern seemed constipated, I added Black Strap Molasses so she could poop comfortably (also a nice source of B vitamins!). When I suspected that the addition of dry gelatin was making her poop a very strange combination of dense and grainy, I omitted it and opted instead to lengthen the time I boiled chicken bones for broth to release naturally occurring gelatin. When the Cod Liver Oil, which contains important omegas and fats for the brain, made Fern smell funny, I thought, "You can't be the kid who has Down syndrome AND smells like fish." So I switched to a more expensive option that did away with the fishy burps.

As promised, Dr. Gastro called with the results of her analysis on the Friday following our visit.

I was eager for the results and did little to hide my excitement. "Hi Dr. Gastro! I've been waiting to hear from you!" I slipped on my headset so I could continue cleaning up after lunch.

Dr. Gastro said, "I have the nutritional analysis ready for you, and it seems like everything looks good. Fern is getting enough calories. There's a perfect balance of fat and protein in the formula you are feeding her. And if you say she's not too gassy or constipated," I could hear her flipping through some papers on the other end, "then I think it's probably working really well for Fern."

I rinsed the remains of a mashed avocado from a plate. Dr. Gastro hadn't said anything to surprise me, and yet I was very reassured by this information.

"Great!" I said, loading the plate into the dishwasher. "I am really glad to hear this."

Dr. Gastro said, "The only minor consideration is that the Vitamin A was a little lower than we usually liked to see for a baby Fern's age."

"Oh, I don't think that's a problem," I said, wiping down the counter as I talked. "Fern is eating sweet potatoes every other day, so she's getting it from food instead."

"There you go then," Dr. Gastro said. "I think you don't have anything to worry about."

I stopped what I was doing. "Thank you. Really, I appreciate this peace of mind."

Dr. Gastro softened her tone. "Ms. House, give her time. Fern started out small and she just had heart surgery. She'll catch up. She just needs a little more time."

I dropped the rag in the sink and leaned against the counter. This is what I had been longing to here.

"Thanks," I said. "I appreciate that perspective. Especially coming from a doctor."

And sure enough, by her next appointment, Fern was on the growth charts. ALL of the growth charts.

EIGHTEEN

Burden on Society

At family gatherings, it was not uncommon to hear members of my family bemoan people who were a burden on society. This sweeping categorization included, but was not limited to, teenage mothers, any one in jail, poor people, drug users, homeless people and "retarded" people who could make no meaningful contribution to society. I didn't know much about politics or the role government could play in a person's life, but even as a young child it was clear to me from the tone of the conversation that being a burden on society was unpardonable. Even as I began to stake out my own identity as a left-leaning, pro-choice environmentalist, I always considered myself a fiscal conservative when it came to government handouts.

Then Fern was born. In the days following her birth and surprise diagnosis, our world came crashing down around us and our dreams for our baby girl suddenly turned nightmarish. Between Fern's extended stay in the NICU and her open heart surgery, a tidal wave of medical expenses was unleashed. Our near future was booked with back to back doctor appointments and the foreseeable future was packed with therapists and evaluations. There were neurologists, cardiologists, ophthalmologists and all sorts of therapists, all enlisted to help our daughter. I found myself asking whether my marriage, our family and our finances could weather this storm. In addition to being emotionally gut wrenching and incredibly disappointing, having a child with Down syndrome sounded...expensive.

Even with our decent insurance through my husband's job, I knew there was plenty of medical expense that would go uncovered as the total raced towards $150,000. So when they sent a social worker around to help answer any questions we might have about Fern's diagnosis, one of my first questions was, "Will this mean financial ruin for my family?"

To my great relief, the social worker calmly and matter-of-factly told me, "No. There are government programs that will help you every step of the way."

I looked at her through puffy eyes. "Every step?" I asked. "We don't have to sell all of our stocks or move out of our house?"

"Every step."

I sighed with relief. At a time when I felt very vulnerable and afraid, a burden of worry had been lifted. And, in accepting this relief, one more burden on society was born.

·　　　　·　　　　·

By the time I sat across from the woman with the distractingly frizzy hair, I was fairly used to feeling vulnerable and unsure. Fern was only three-weeks-old but, thanks to her diagnosis, I was getting used to being at the mercy of a stranger who has the knowledge or skill or power to help my child. But, just three weeks into our "new normal," I was also starting to understand that we didn't have to accept all the help that was being offered.

As I took her in, I started to regret ever having agreed to this meeting. She wore no makeup, and her face could have been kind had it ever been allowed to bask in a little sunshine or joy. Her clothes, like much about her, were forgettable. Tidy and therefore beyond reproach. She wore no accessories other than her name tag, which read "WIC Coordinator, Susan Triggs," and a strand of colorful beads hanging around her neck. They sparkled playfully in the drab light one expects from a government office, but even these were assigned the pragmatic task of keeping her reading glasses close.

Susan turned primly in my direction and explained, "Because of Fern's diagnosis, you qualify for federal aid to supplement your dietary needs through the program called Women, Infants and Children, also known as WIC."

This meant that once every few months, I could show up at the WIC office with Fern in tow and, after a weigh in and short evaluation, I could leave with checks to buy food designated to help me and Fern meet our nutritional needs for the coming three months. Fern's diagnosis guaranteed her participation in the program for the next five years, whereas I would only receive checks for one year.

Days prior, in an effort to convince my husband that visiting the WIC office was a waste of time, I asked, "What does having a child who has special needs have to do with being poor? Fern might have had Down syndrome, but we can feed our children, and probably do a damn better job than any government program!"

"That's probably true," Will countered, "but we should still look into it."

"Doesn't it seem silly to offer us assistance just because our kid had special needs? Isn't this is a clear indication that the system of government handouts is really screwed up?"

Will shrugged. "I don't want to make any decisions until we have all the information."

Will spent the first nine years of his life sometimes homeless and often hungry. He's the kind of guy if you give him a dollar on Tuesday and check back with him on Friday, he has a dollar and a quarter. He doesn't like to spend money and he always takes any help that is offered. I admire Will's penny-pinching, make-do attitude and his willingness to accept help when it's offered. I assume these traits helped him get off the streets and become the healthy, well-liked, self-sufficient adult that he is.

But Will wasn't being offered the WIC assistance. I was, because I was the "W" in Women Infants and Children. And it felt yucky. It was only at Will's insistence that I agreed to swallow my considerable pride and check it out. So there I was managing my twins, who at three-weeks-old weighed a collective eleven pounds, sitting across from Susan, who was there to "educate" me about my options, while my mom entertained Cypress in the lobby.

Susan continued, "Additionally, according to the paychecks you provided, Sylvan and Cypress are also qualified to receive WIC checks."

"Wait. I thought we were here because Fern has Down syndrome. I'm not even sure what you are saying." The woman took off her glasses and let them dangle from the strand of beads. She showed me the worksheet she had just completed.

"Your income level is such that you and your three children are eligible to receive WIC checks. Would you like to enroll all of your children in the program now?"

I leaned forward to see the worksheet. "Are you saying we don't just qualify because Fern has Down syndrome? That we also qualify because we are legitimately poor?"

I was stunned. I knew things were tight, but I also knew that I was living the life I wanted to live. Staying home with my children felt like my highest calling. If it meant not having a cell phone (I didn't) or paying for expensive entertainment options (we didn't own a tv with cable, and we canceled Netflix and date nights), or limiting the trips I took in our very used vehicles to stretch our gas budget, so be it. Even with a tight budget, we ate better than most of the American population. Not just in quantity, but in quality. We kept a large garden and ate very little processed foods. I was living my dream. It wasn't easy, but it sure beat sitting at a computer all day making someone else rich.

It never occurred to me that we might actually be part of "working poor" class and I felt humiliated.

·   ·   ·

We left the WIC office and my mom offered to buy a late breakfast. It had been a depressing visit and I was turning things over in my head. How did I, organizer of all things, become so entangled with the government, giant of all things inefficient? In the last couple of weeks, my self-image had made a terrifying transformation from "Confident Stay at Home Mother" to "Loser Lowlife Mother of a Child with Special Needs."

My mom bit into her cinnamon roll and asked me, "So, what'd you think of the other people at the WIC office?"

"You mean the other moms?" I had confessed a deep dread of sharing the lobby with women who smelled like stale cigarettes surrounded by grubby, blank-faced children. "Actually, they were fine. I guess they were a lot like me. They seemed pretty normal."

My mom took a sip of her coffee. "And did you find the staff patronizing." Another concern I had confided.

"No." If there had been the slightest hint of "Say please!" I would have left without a word. But everyone was courtesy and the only command was, "Sign here, please."

"And does that make you feel differently about accepting help?"

"Mom, I don't want to be the person who qualifies for federal aid."

"I know, but why not take the help that's being offered?"

"Because it's gross, and I'll just be another loser lining up for a hand out."

"Heather, not everyone who needs help is a loser. You aren't a loser and you don't get points for making things harder for yourself."

"Yeah, but I don't like feeling like I'm part of a bigger problem"

The thing that galled me was that I realized we actually had to make a choice. When Susan outlined the kinds of food we could buy with WIC checks, I knew Will would want to sign up. We could get beans and tofu, cheese and tortillas. Things we ate. We could turn the milk (which we don't drink) into Greek-style yogurt (which we love). And who was I to argue? I could either accept the help, which would make our lives a small measure easier, or deny it out of pride and principle.

"I just wish we had more money and I didn't have to think about it. I feel like there are no good options. I could go back to work and spend thousands of dollars per month to pay someone else to care for my kids, or I can stay poor and accept government assistance." I sighed, feeling sorry for myself and like I didn't have much to offer the world. Trying to bring some levity to the situation, I said, "Maybe I could make some quick cash by selling my eggs."

My mom rolled her eyes. "Heather, you're forty-years-old and you've just given birth to a kid with Down syndrome. Nobody wants your eggs."

·   ·   ·

In the end, we accepted the WIC help. Other than showing up for quarterly meetings, I was largely uninvolved. This was due in part to my considerable pride, but more directly because I was still nursing and pumping for twin infants. I rarely left the house and I certainly did not take on as complicated a task as grocery shopping.

Although the other moms in the WIC program were nothing like I expected (they were often married graduate students), the office was just as dismal as I had imagined it would be. We sat knee-to-knee in a windowless waiting area, surrounded by dingy walls decorated with bland government posters. The process was tedious and confusing, and there was repetitive paperwork to be filled out. Undoubtedly, there was a real effort to make the WIC program accessible and easy, but it was an effort mandated by a cumbersome bureaucracy.

And Susan ran the show. There was something about Susan, about how she could only move in a very predictable, forward manner following scripts written by authorities far removed from the population they served. She was courteous enough, but had her office been a business they would have long suffered from poor customer service reviews. It rankled me to know that in another setting I could run circles around this woman, that I did more in a morning with three small children than she did all week but that, when I set foot in that office, I was on her turf, moving at her snail's pace, confined within her rigid, precise boundaries. It wasn't that I didn't like her; I just didn't understand her. Our visits were always a little tense, tinged with something like begrudged deference.

The food one can purchase with WIC is…adequate. Most of our gripes were the kind you might expect from once-middle class white people with advanced degrees. We were able to trade a little extra cheese for less milk, but we were leery of bringing non-organic milk into our home. We were glad to see tofu on the list, bummed that the only brand match we could find was always silken, never firm. We picked up all the jars of baby food allotted to us thinking that one day we'd get a great idea for how to feed them to our babies, but it was just too much and we ended up giving most of it away to people who really needed it. We were happy there was $15 allocated toward fresh fruits and vegetables every month, but we easily consumed that much in three or four days.

During our short stint on WIC, it seemed we always had corn tortillas in the fridge and juice in the cabinet, high calories treats we rarely ate before WIC. But we made the best of it and shifted our eating habits to accommodate the WIC foods. We ate a lot of quesadillas, which were both fast and filling, and we came up with all kinds of tricks for using up the canned tuna and salmon. I joked that we should start a blog with recipes that featured WIC products and call it WICked Good.

We learned a lot by being on WIC for a year. It seems the program is set up in a way that affords the user a certain degree of dignity. The powerlessness one feels around needing, or simply qualifying for, assistance is offset by the choices one is offered within the program. We weren't allowed to buy exactly what we wanted, but neither were we forced to accept whatever they handed us. We could choose between x and y, or substitute z. We had choice, albeit limited, and choice is power.

Most of the time, Will came home from grocery shopping with WIC checks saying, "You gotta be smart if you're gonna be poor!"

Figuring out exactly, and I mean *exactly,* which products are allowed to be purchased with WIC checks is not easy. Standing in the grocery aisle with his full color brochure in hand, Will could spend 20 minutes trying to find the right bag of beans. You could get the blue brand, but only in a 16 ounce, which the store did not carry. They might have the 16 ounce in the red brand, but WIC only allowed the 20 ounce for the red brand. Okay, no beans this week. But wait. Now that he was in the international section, he spots the yellow brand in a 16 ounce package and BINGO! It matches the WIC check and beans are back on the menu!

But that was only half the battle. If there was a system error at check out and the UPC code was not recognized by the store as a WIC product, anything could happen. Will could argue until he was blue in the face, pointing to the brochure and perfectly aligned product in hand, and a certain manager would just shake their head and say, "Nope. The system says it is not acceptable. Sorry." Another manager might look at the same situation and say, "I'm so sorry for your trouble. Yes, that should work just fine. Let me fix that in the system so you don't have that same problem next time." Ultimately, the store with the nicest managers won our business and we still shop there today.

After being on the program for a year, it was time to resubmit paperwork and once again, Susan pulled out her income calculation worksheet. The twins had just turned one, so Sylvan crawled and cruised around the room while Fern, who could finally sit on her own, watched. Cypress played with the magnets on the side of Susan's desk and I sat in my seat wondering how many times a day Susan filled out that same worksheet and how it was possible she never got any faster at it.

When she was done with her worksheet, Susan turned it to me so I could see the results as she informed me, "It looks like your husband has received a raise. So now only Fern qualifies. You and your other children will no longer receive WIC checks."

I hadn't expected this and I had mixed feelings. Yes, it was true that Will had received a raise. A very *modest* one and so I hardly felt like we were better off. It put us just over the WIC qualification line, and suddenly the line felt very arbitrary. And yet, it also seemed right, as I never thought we should qualify in the first place. We were doing fine before WIC. In truth, I liked the way we ate better before WIC came along. But still. There was no question that WIC checks had helped and our food budget was much more manageable.

Since we were already over run with baby food and had no intention of feeding our babies homogenized, pasteurized, non-organic milk, we did not enroll Fern for another year. I appreciated the assistance, but I like retaining control over what my babies ate even more.

I was relieved to be free of the WIC program, but also greatly humbled by the experience. For the first time, I saw how close we were living to the edge. Logically, I knew we were fine and could continue caring for our kids, as we had been living off a single modest income for years. And we had family who could help us if our world came crashing down. But now I had a very clear understanding that many people were living just one bad accident away from true poverty. Hell, if it weren't for the government programs that paid for Fern's time in the NICU and the heart surgery, we would already be bankrupt. So even as I kissed Susan and her prissy unbending ways goodbye, I sent up a little prayer of gratitude up for a government that is there to catch us when we fall.

NINETEEN

Early Intervention

To have a child who receives the services of Early Intervention is to know the meaning of "mixed feelings." No one wants to be the family who has to schedule play dates around therapy appointments, but if you have a child with special needs, you might consider the appointments a highlight of your week. It's no fun knowing your child has to be taught how to put weight on her feet or make verbal responses to mothering coos, but it's encouraging to have professionals who love showing her how.

Two or three times a week, one of Fern's cheerful, competent therapists knocks on our door around 8 A.M. to work one-on-one with Fern for 60-90 minutes. Sylvan runs to the door to greet them and fill them in on the news of the morning. "Charlene! Dad made oatmeal and I have new shoes!" "Maria! We were looking for your blue car and I got myself dressed!"

For all the hang ups I had about accepting help from WIC, I couldn't wait to get started with Early Intervention, whose therapists' salaries, like WIC, are paid for by our collective tax dollars. I was pretty sure I didn't need government help to feed my kids, but I didn't know the first thing about physical, occupational, speech or cognitive therapies and there was no way we could afford those therapies out of pocket.

Whereas the concept of Early Intervention (EI) which has had an enormous impact on the functioning levels of people with special needs, was new and barely understood 40 years ago, in the days following Fern's birth and diagnosis, service providers practically fell over themselves to make sure Fern received services early, often and with as little effort as possible on my part.

One of the more disturbing things about receiving government services is that your child has to fail tests to qualify. This is nothing new for us. When Fern was just six days old, floppy as a rag doll, we knew she could never pass the car seat test administered to every infant before they can be discharged from the hospital. The purpose of the test is to see if a child can sit buckled in a car seat for a full hour and breathe without losing oxygen efficiency. We knew that Fern's hypotonia meant that she would just crumple into a ball when set upright, crushing her windpipe and essentially suffocating her. Everyone knew she would need to come home in a car bed (like a car seat, but only laying down), so it wasn't a question of whether or not she would pass or fail the test. As with the EI services, what we really needed to know was just how bad she would fail.

It is one thing to know your child isn't able to do something, and it's another thing to watch them be set up to systematically fail to quantify their lacking. In the three short years we've known Fern, we have signed dozens of consent forms for well-meaning professionals to administer one test or another for Fern to fail, documenting she needs one service or another. It's the nature of the game and I try to take it in stride, but it's hard to see your kid, who you want to believe is bright and capable and making great progress, fail to do the most simple of tasks. Times like this, I draw heavily on the wisdom of my friend Lucey, Lili's mom, who once told me that she stopped looking at milestones and test results and instead just asked, "What's the next thing I should be watching for Lili to do and how can I help her do it?"

That's where the services of EI have been like salve on a wound. EI is founded on a simple tenant: kids like Fern can learn, especially if we break the learning down into smaller pieces. EI therapists are expert in breaking the learning down into tiny pieces and they know how to identify the next micro-step. For example, finger pinching comes before using two hands in opposition, which is followed by the use of utensils, which requires practice of eye-hand coordination, which is necessary for using scissors. Skills like these emerge naturally for a typically developing kid who is allowed to explore her world, but we need to set an intention to *teach* these things to a kid with development delays so that these skills can emerge sooner and the child can gain proficiency faster. The job of the therapist is less about teaching Fern specific skills and more about teaching us, her parents, how to work with Fern. It's like dog-training, in that the skills taught to the dog are only as good as the owner's ability to reinforce them.

For example, Fern's speech therapist came armed with all sorts of ideas to help Fern communicate, chief among them using baby signs. We had used sign language to communicate with Cypress, so we thought using sign language with Fern would be a no brainer. But like many of our best laid plans for Fern, she had her own ideas about communicating. Once we were at the beach when a helicopter started approaching from the west. As it traveled along the shore, the boys were yelling "Helicopter! Helicopter!" I seized the moment to teach Fern our made-up sign for helicopter, a splayed hand making small circular motions parallel to the ground like the blades of a helicopter. Fern had a shovel in each of her hands and as the helicopter got closer she quickly transferred the shovel in her right hand to her left hand. Grasping both shovels with her left hand, I thought she had freed the right hand to make the sign I had just shown her. Instead, as the helicopter flew past us, she pointed with her right hand and said excitedly, "Dat-waz-a-copter!" That was a 'copter.

But Fern is nothing if not inconsistent, and this is what trips me up over and over again. The boys started communicating with simple signs, followed by simple words, then two-word phrases and so on. Their learning is a clear trajectory, one that does not deviate much from the millions of books written on the subject of child development. With Fern, one day she signed "more," and we jumped for joy, then just a few weeks later she pointed at a cage in the zoo and correctly pronounced, "This is a black bear!" Then she went silent and didn't say anything recognizable for days. It made no sense, and it defied everything we had been told to expect from a kid with Down syndrome. Fern's speech therapist was there every step of the way cheering for Fern and encouraging us to keep doing what was working and try new ways of communicating with our smart little girl.

I think every parent gets something different out of EI. For me, their mere presence in my small rural home helps life feels a little less isolating, like I'm not the only mom out there trying to figure this thing out. My loyalty to the therapist motivates me to work with Fern. With an almost childish desire to please, I want to show them that Fern is making progress, that their time spent in our home is worthwhile. Knowing they have decades of experience working with a wide range of challenges helps me keep my perspective, too. We could be dealing with much, much bigger challenges. Some of the kids our same therapists work with will *never* walk or talk or feed themselves.

Then there is the moral support. EI therapists would never discuss the details of another client's progress, but when I start to feel a little sad about Fern losing ground, they make a point of telling me that Fern is remarkable. I might mention how distressing it is to see one of Fern's peers with Down syndrome is able to do something she can't yet do, like sing his ABC's, and they will remind me of one of her strengths and point out, for example, that most of her peers have yet to poop on the potty. And if the wind goes out of my sails a little when Sylvan plays the memory game and Fern still just throws the cards on the floor, they remind me that some of Fern's three year-old peers still haven't taken their first steps while Fern is able to climb UP the slide. Their perspective is an encouraging antidote to my cynicism.

The thing you will never get from EI is a permanent solution to the underlying issue. They aren't there to "fix" anything. After our first visit from an EI therapist, I felt deflated. For all their enthusiasm and all their good ideas, I saw clearly that the burden of helping Fern meet her potential was going to fall to me. I was already feeling pretty overwhelmed as a stay-at-home mom to three kids under the age of two. On the best days, it was pure unadulterated chaos bordering on hell. On the bad days, well, don't even ask. Between nursing Sylvan, pumping breast milk for Fern, and potty training 22-month old Cypress, there wasn't even time for a good cry. How was I going to work therapy into this mess?

As usual, the answer is simple: I have to stop thinking of Fern's progress as a checklist of goals or a competition we're trying to win. Although we might not be able to give Fern the individualized attention she needs (let's face it, no one in this family is getting the all the individualized attention they "need"), with modifications, we can work practicing a certain skill or task into daily life. In the beginning, we learned the art of propping Fern on her belly with rolled up receiving blankets. We never did that exercise again until the next time our physical therapy session, but Fern got plenty of opportunities to be on her belly and strengthen her neck when I carried her around the house in the football hold. Later, when she could sit up, I found myself helping Fern get into trouble. She couldn't crawl, but she was ready for the cognitive development that happens when you pull mommy's Tupperware out of the cabinet. And when it seemed like it might be beneficial for Fern to take gymnastics class to build hand and arm strength, I almost had a panic attack at the thought of spending an hour getting three kids ready and driving into town to attend a 45 minute class with other insane toddlers. Instead, I ordered a trapeze bar with rings and hung it from our living room ceiling next to a used child-size trampoline I bought from a Facebook friend. All of the kids, including Fern, hang and jump whenever they want to, and they are all noticeably stronger (and I am noticeably saner) for it. And never underestimate the motivation of siblings! When Fern's speech therapist taught me how to end a little song one beat early, pausing to let Fern finish the song, I turned around and taught the song and little trick of pausing to let Fern finish it to Sylvan and Cypress, who happily sang the mind-numbing tune with Fern over and over again.

•   •   •

As Fern's third birthday approaches, I can feel our relationship with the EI therapists has started to shift. When she turns three, Intermediate Unit services will pick up where EI services end and we are gearing up for that transition. It is a bittersweet time. These women have been a huge part of our journey and we will miss them terribly. I'm one of those housekeepers who you can tell how much I like you by how messy my house is when you come over. The messier it is, the more comfortable I am with our friendship. Fern's therapists are the kind of people for whom I might pick up dirty underwear but feel no obligation to clean up the breakfast dishes.

At our last quarterly review, all four of Fern's therapists, plus her service coordinator, a therapist in training, her future service coordinator and me, gathered together to discuss Fern's progress. They took turns updating the group on whether Fern has made progress toward the goals we have set, saying things like, "She's doing so great!" and "She's blowing my mind." Throughout the meeting, even though Fern's 3rd birthday is months away, I got the sense that Fern's therapists feel their work is done and the consensus is that Fern is going to be just fine. We spent the hour talking about statistics, average age of potty training, average number or words in phrases she can/should use, how to best handle the transition to preschool, etc. It's all good and important, and I appreciate the enthusiasm of Fern's EI team. As a team, we have worked hard to bring out the best in Fern, and that's worthy of celebration. Out of respect for them, and because no one wants to be the sad mom, I smiled and nodded and agreed that yes, Fern is amazing and, yes, the upcoming transition is exciting.

But once they left my reality came rushing back in. We have the control group living in our home. Sylvan might be off the charts in the other direction, brilliant even, but the difference between Fern and Sylvan is more than just a few IQ points. Fern talks more than most kids her age who have Down syndrome but she can only say about a 10th of what Sylvan can and only people who know her well can understand what she is saying. The reason Fern doesn't recount the events of the day or tell elaborate stories like her brother isn't solely because she doesn't have the words for it; it's also because she's not thinking about those things yet. Fern's typical sibling is leaving her in the dust and, perverse as it may be, I'm almost outraged by her therapists' glee.

The thing is, when you have a kid who has special needs, you don't suddenly wake up and find you've come to terms with it, unflappable and able to celebrate that kid for exactly who they are. I have to come to terms with it over and over again as I understand on a deeper and deeper level that this isn't a problem we solve once and move on from. No matter how great your team of therapists, no matter how intentional you are about working therapies into the daily routine, the underlying issues remains the same: my kid has an extra chromosome and, therefore, a lifetime of extra challenges.

I remember the doctor who delivered Fern's diagnosis telling me that the only way we would truly understand the severity of Fern's disability would be when she showed us what she could and could not do. Meaning, given the wide range of abilities of people who have Down syndrome, we could only guess at what the future held. The best thing to do, they said, was to take it day by day and let Fern show us, over time, what she was capable of doing. Most days, I'm okay with this. But every now and then, I look ahead and see with great clarity the road ahead of us and it is paved with endless problem solving. And for every bump that is another test Fern has failed, there will be a therapist trying to smooth the ride, assuring us with their characteristic reckless enthusiasm that Fern is doing great.

This thing with Fern is not as crushing as it used to be, and I've gotten better about not comparing Fern to other kids, especially her twin. It doesn't happen as often as it used to, and I recover a lot faster than I did at the beginning, but I sometimes I come up against the reality of Fern and it is like a slap in the face.

So yeah, Fern is doing great. She's probably even amazing. She really is…for a kid who has Down syndrome.

TWENTY

Pears

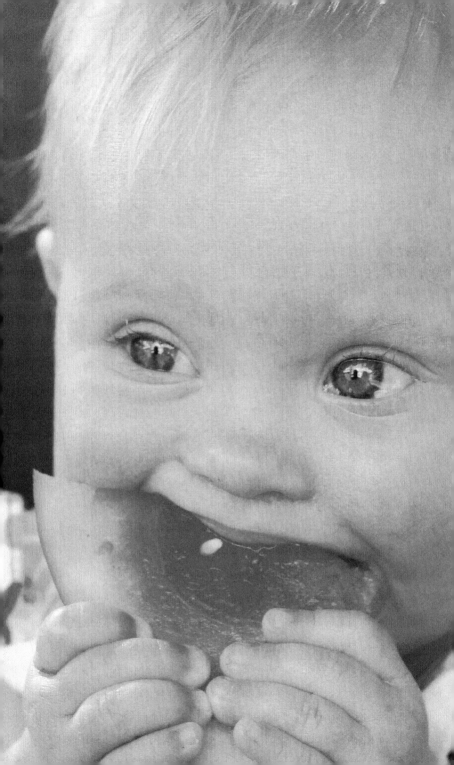

When I think of how people with Down syndrome used to be institutionalized, it is the knowledge that these children and adults were perfectly aware of what was going on around them, perfectly able to learn, that breaks my heart. All that untapped potential, all that learned helplessness.

Not that I'm going to win any awards for always being attuned to Fern's potential.

On the day I chose for Sylvan's "first food" milestone, I strapped a bib around his neck, popped open a jar of pears and got the camera ready in hopes of catching a cute picture. Sylvan had four teeth and showed all the classic signs of being ready to supplement nursing with solid food. He sat on his own, watched intently as food move from our plates to our mouths, and reached for food on our plates. Meanwhile, Fern only sat when propped by rolled towels in her Bumbo and she seemed content to play while we ate.

I offered Sylvan his first bite of baby food on the end of a rubber-tipped spoon. He was interested, but he couldn't get the knack of moving food to the back of his mouth with his tongue and food gushed out of his mouth when he tried to swallow. Teaching babies to eat is a painful, time-consuming task, I find, and I started to feel a little deflated as reality set in. It would be weeks before Sylvan would polish off a jar of baby food, and months before he was competent enough to feed himself.

Then I noticed Fern was watching me from her Bumbo, intensely curious about what was happening.

I asked her, "You want to try some pears, baby girl?"

I strapped a bib around her neck and parked her Bumbo next to Sylvan. Then I scooped up a spoonful of pears and coaxed her mouth open to accept the spoon. She looked at me wide-eyed, but once she got a taste of pears the rest came naturally. Oh, her tongue flipped and flailed, thrusted and twisted the way the tongues of babies with Down syndrome will do, but somehow she figured it out. After just a couple of tries, Fern swallowed most of the food I put into her mouth. She happily accepted mouthful after mouthful of pears, smacking her lips and opening her mouth for more.

The now-familiar feeling of mama guilt started rising in my chest. Why did I assume that Fern couldn't do something when I hadn't even given her a chance to try? How many times per day did the "Fern Has Down syndrome" filter negatively affect the way I parent Fern? How often did I lower my expectations for Fern, thereby depriving her of the chance to stretch to her full potential? Would I ever be able to read the milestone readiness signals from Fern the way I could read my other two?

When I called my mom to tell her about Fern's triumph, I said, "Mom, she's such a tidy eater, much neater than Sylvan! She takes clean bites and hardly drips any on her bib. I can't believe she's a kid with Down syndrome!"

"Well, Heather," my mom said, "She's not just a kid with Down syndrome, you know. You're going to have to get used to the fact that she's also lady-like."

Yes, Fern could be lady-like, though that's not exactly the word I would use to describe our adventures in potty-training.

It started when Will was out of town on a business trip and my mom was staying with me to help with the kids. Fern was naked, ready for bath time, but the bath water was too hot. I needed to set her down someplace so I could adjust the water temperature. At 16 months old, Fern still could not stand, (in fact, she wouldn't even put weight on her feet), and I feared the bathroom tiles were too cold for her naked bum, so I set her on the child's potty next to the tub. By the time I had turned off the hot water and reached down to pick up Fern, she'd pooped in the potty! My mom and I both gasped, then started laughing.

"She's so smart!" my mom declared.

I said, "I'm calling Will."

Every night after that, we sat Fern on the potty just before bath time and every night she pooped and every night Will called to hear about this amazing feat. Was this potty training? Or was this just good timing? It didn't matter, as Fern could not walk, much less manage the fine motor skills required for removing her clothes to get to the potty. In short, I was still managing her excrement.

It's been nearly a year since Fern started pooping on the potty. Now she can walk. She even has the necessary language to communicate the act of peeing (she grabs her diaper and says Peh Peh). With the addition of an extra piece of Velcro, she can manage the fine motor skills necessary to remove her diaper. It's just a matter of getting it all together, which feels like it might take an eternity. Let me tell you, you haven't lived until you've picked up a six inch turd off the public library floor. Follow that with a frantic search up and down the book aisles for the diaper your child with fine motor "impairment" managed to rip off and you've got yourself some real entertainment!

It's easy to use Fern's diagnosis as an excuse for delaying potty training. I hate potty training. Fern is probably ready, but I'm dragging my feet. There's no way this will be as easy at potty training Sylvan, who basically potty-trained himself in a matter of days. But then, there were some problems with that too.

Sylvan saw his older brother Cypress using the potty and he was determined to do the same. Before he was even two-years old he started refusing to wear a diaper and insisted on using the potty. And almost immediately he was sleeping through the night dry. The problem was he climbed out of his crib at 5:00 am to pee on the floor and then could not climb back into his crib. After a couple of early mornings trying to get him to the potty before he peed and then pleading with him (unsuccessfully) to go back to bed, we decided it was time to convert his crib to a toddler bed.

Fern watched us and played with the wrenches alongside the boys as Will removed one of the side rails from Sylvan's crib. Fern celebrated her twin's newfound freedom by squealing with delight and flailing her body on the mattress through the now-open side. Then she turned and did the same on Cypress's bed, and I understood what she understood: Sylvan's bed matched their older brother's. Sylvan was now a big boy.

Then we put the tools away. That night, Fern protested when we put her in her crib and I understood that, like so many things, she wanted what the boys had, wanted to do what the boys were doing. I just didn't feel she was ready. She was a long way from showing any of the "typical" signs of being ready for a toddler bed. She was barely walking, much less climbing. There was absolutely no threat of her climbing out of her crib. She still wore a diaper and that was wet in the morning. There wasn't any compelling reason to transition Fern to a toddler bed and, frankly, I wasn't sure she could handle the responsibility.

But, she clearly wanted what the boys had. Bed time became a struggle that included time for her to protest her crib each night. The fact that Fern is perfectly attuned to injustices is a source of pride for me. It's a reflection of how our family culture is to include her in everything. Even though it requires extra effort, from the very beginning I never let Fern sit outside the circle of what we were doing as a family. Even if she seem content laying on the floor in the living room, if we were all in the playroom I picked her up and moved her close to us. When Sylvan gained the trunk strength to sit in highchair clipped to the table and Fern still needed to be propped in a Bumbo with towels, I moved Fern and her Bumbo to the middle of the dining room table. Until she learned to crawl and could choose where she wanted to be, I spent a lot of time moving her to where the boys were playing. The intended message was, "You are part of our family. You are to be included in everything we do. You are wanted."

After a few weeks of protesting her crib, I decided to give her a shot at the big girl bed. Here is the Facebook post from the morning after we took the railing off her crib:

A little bed-head pic to celebrate a huge milestone for this big girl! Fern slept in her toddler bed for the first time last night, and did not fall out! More impressive is that, even though she was heady with all the freedom, she listened when we told her she needed to get in bed and stay in bed. She put her head on her pillow and stayed there until she fell asleep. She was the first one up banging on the bedroom door to get up, but I called our usual morning chant from bed, "You gotta wait for 'green light wake up,' Fern!" and off she toddled back to her bed to wait for the alarm clock light to change. Seriously, this is as much a parenting milestone for me as it is a big girl milestone for Fern. I had my doubts. I wondered how many times she would have to fall out of bed before she gained that subtle body awareness required to stay on an elevated platform through the night. I wondered how much she could understand about staying in bed and how much responsibility she could handle. But given the opportunity, this girl shines, shines, shines!

TWENTY-ONE

Meeting People Who Have Down Syndrome

When is it okay to ask whether someone has Down syndrome? What *is* the protocol here? I mean, when are you ever truly 100% certain? And what if you're wrong? How do you politely say, "My bad, you look like someone who has developmental delays?"

I speak a little Japanese and there was a time when I was eager to practice any chance I got. One time, my husband and I were at a noodle house in central Pennsylvania and I swore the couple next to me was speaking Japanese.

"So talk to them," my husband prodded.

I listened carefully, but could only make out a few familiar sounds.

"They are talking so fast. I can't make out what they are saying," I said. "I think I'm getting rusty."

"Well, now's your chance to get some practice," Will said.

"Good point."

I poked my head around the corner and said in shaky Japanese, "Excuse me, are you speaking Japanese?"

The couple gave me a confused look. Thinking my Japanese had gotten really bad, I switched to English, "Are you speaking Japanese?"

They looked at each other with raised eyebrows, and then the woman said to me in carefully pronounced English, "We are Korean."

And I am an idiot.

Still, mistaking a Korean person for a Japanese person, while potentially offensive, is a pardonable sin. While living in Japan, I myself had to forgive many Japanese who mistook me for Meg Ryan or a Canadian. These things happen. But mistaking a "normal" person for a person with special needs? Well, as politically incorrect as it may be to say, I think that just crosses a line.

So I surprise even myself sometimes with my nerve sometimes. Whereas I once would have changed checkout lanes at the grocery store to avoid having to come in contact with a person who has special needs, I now go out of my way to meet people I notice who have Down syndrome.

Once I was driving down Main Street in a small town and a noticed a man who had Down syndrome unloading groceries from the back of a car. I whipped an illegal u-turn, parked next to the car and got out to introduce myself.

Another time I casually followed a man who had Down syndrome in a grocery store until I got up the nerve to introduce myself to him and his mother. A few weeks later, I saw them at our local Down syndrome group's holiday party and we said hi like we were old friends!

On vacation in Florida, I walked up to a woman with Down syndrome who appeared to be shopping on her own and introduced myself, then showed her Fern on my back. She did not respond, so I thought perhaps she was non-verbal. I just smiled and repeated, "This is my little girl, she has Down syndrome too." Still no response. I was smiling and thinking I should just walk away when the woman said, "I'm sorry. English is my second language."

I have jumped over ticket gates, scheduled hair appointments for times when an employee who has Down syndrome might be on the clock, and invited myself to join a family for dinner at Chik-Fil-A when I noticed their son had Down syndrome. The outsider might think I'm obsessed. I prefer to think of myself as friendly. In reality, my need to interact with adults who have Down syndrome comes from being an experiential learner. I can't just read books or listen to the passionate testimony of their parents. I need to shake their hands, ask them about their lives, be reassured that they feel happy and fulfilled. I need living examples to show me Fern is going to be okay.

There is a lot of excitement around the Emmy Award winning reality television show *Born This Way*, which features several adults who have Down syndrome trying to make their dreams come true. Some applaud the show for giving real-life examples of what people who have Down syndrome can do with their lives. Others criticize the show for featuring only very high-functioning people which sets unrealistic expectations for people who aren't doing as well. I ran into a couple of adults who have Down syndrome at the pool recently and after some pleasantries I said, "Listen, I have to ask. Do you like *Born This Way*?"

The young woman said, "My mom watches it. But I can't watch it."

"Oh? Why not?" I asked.

"It makes me uncomfortable. It's too much drama."

"That's exactly why I can't watch it!" I exclaimed. "I feel like I should watch it, so I get a sense of what is possible for Fern's future, but I don't like the drama."

The young man agreed. "It is probably a good show for some people. But I don't watch it either."

I said, "Well, maybe you guys can be the ones to show Fern what's possible." They both just nodded, then turned to start a game of peek-a-boo with Fern.

I never know exactly what adults with Down syndrome understand when I banter with them, so I was surprised when the young man called to Fern as we walked away, "Don't worry! You've got us!! We'll show you what you can do!" I mean, you can't make this stuff up. I wanted to happy cry.

Still, I really need to work on my introduction. It always goes better if I have Fern with me, because she obviously has Down syndrome and she is ridiculously cute, which lends certain credibility to my enthusiasm. But even then, I can come on a little strong.

Once I accosted person with Down syndrome at the Farmer's Market. She was with her father and I interrupted the friend I was chatting with saying, "Sorry. I have to go meet those people." I scurried up with Sylvan holding one hand, Fern in the backpack on my back, groceries in the other hand and Cypress tagging on my heels. "Hi! I'm Heather and this is my little girl Fern," I said, swinging around to show them the child on my back. "She has Down syndrome too!"

The woman and her father stared at me, uncomfortable smiles plastered on their faces.

Oh shit. This woman does not have Down syndrome.

Her dad gave me a polite smile, "Hello. I'm David."

I leaned in, "I'm sorry, David. I'm such a spazz. This is Fern. And your daughter...DS, right?"

He nodded, 'Uh, yeah."

"Hi!" I said again, loud like I am when I'm unsure of how to act. "This is Fern. She's has Down syndrome too. What's your name?"

The woman was smiling and now there was no question in my mind that she had Down syndrome. I wondered if she was verbal. She looked like she wanted to fold in on herself. She mumbled something and I looked to her father for interpretation.

"Lydia," he said.

"Hi Lydia! How old are you?" I guessed her to be about 19.

"I'm thirty three. But I'm going to be thirty four next March."

I was seven years older than Lydia, but it felt more like twenty. "Great! I loved my thirties!"

I still don't know how to act around adults with Down syndrome. Think about your thirties. At 30 I was living with my boyfriend, and before the decade was up we would buy a house, change jobs, get married and have three children. Now think about Lydia's thirties. She probably still lives with her parents (well, maybe you did too).

Lydia was wearing a giant sparkly flower headband, a striped sparkly over shirt, wild pants, and glittery Mary Janes. In short, she was dressed like a 9-year-old.

"I love your style!" I said, and she lit up. It's something I would say to any thirty year-old who made an obvious effort at fashion, but I had to work to use my not-condescending voice when I said it to Lydia. Later, when I was undressing for bed, I realized that while I was feeling sad thinking that Fern, too, might dress like a 9-year-old when she was 30, I had been wearing a cartooned *Super Mario Brothers* baby tee and a glitter-coated bobby pin in my hair.

I asked, "Where do you live?"

She answered, "Woodward."

And suddenly I was overdoing it again, gushing "I love Woodward! We live in Centre Hall."

Then there was an awkward pause.

"This is Fern! She has Down syndrome too!" I know I've already said it, but I have somehow chosen the path of "idiot" and seem determined to blaze down it.

I asked, "Are you guys involved with the Centre County Down syndrome Society?" and I could see by the way Tom shook his head that people like me are precisely why they are not involved.

I embarrassed myself for another minute or so, then I said, "Well, I'm sorry I just came on so strong. I have three kids and it makes me act a little crazy." This is a blatant lie because as anyone who knows me well can tell you, this is just the sort of stupid thing I was doing long before my kids came along.

We said goodbye and I had a good laugh about my weirdo-tendencies with the very friend I'd just ditched. I felt a bit disappointed because I really like connecting with parents of adults who have Down syndrome. They are generally pretty upbeat and helpful. I kind of consider the fact that we have children who have Down syndrome automatic admission to an exclusive club, a privilege we should somehow bond over. But I didn't think David and I were going to be in any club together. In fact, I was pretty sure David was going to pretend he didn't remember who I was if we should happen to run into each other again.

But later that day, I actually did run into David and Lydia again. I had just arrived at the grocery store and, once again, I had one kid on my back, one in my right arm, and one holding my left hand when David and Lydia drove up in their pickup. David rolled down the window and said, "Keep that up and you're going to need another arm!" I laughed, then I looked at Lydia and said, "Hi again!" She threw me a big smile and David drove off with a wave.

I walked into the store with a self-satisfied smile because I knew, without a doubt, that I was in. We might not have a monthly meeting or pay quarterly dues, but the very exclusive Down syndrome Club of Woodward had just admitted its newest member.

TWENTY-TWO

Do I Have to be an Advocate?

Just a month or so after Fern and Sylvan were born, the local Down syndrome society threw a summer potluck picnic. I was nervous about attending, but I was hoping to meet two other new moms I'd heard about whose daughters were born within days of Fern.

Upon arriving at the picnic, we felt like celebrities. Everyone seemed to know we were coming with newborn twins and that Fern was very tiny. Everyone we met was so kind and welcoming, but they also seemed to understand that we were feeling overwhelmed and afraid. They gave us plenty of space, even as they ooh-ed and ahh-ed at the babies while Cypress had a blast playing with the older kids on the playground.

Looking back, I can understand why the other new mothers, who were no-shows, decided they weren't ready for this kind of thing yet. It was pretty intense. As kind as all the seasoned parents were, it was difficult to look around the picnic and see Fern's future. With at least 20 people who had Down syndrome in attendance, both children and adults, here was a wide range of possible outcomes for Fern, and none of them looked good to me. It seemed like everyone with Down syndrome was overweight, talked funny, and dressed poorly.

Pointing at a little girl I judged to be around five years old, I asked someone, "How old is that little girl over there?" I was stunned when they told me she was nine! She was uncoordinated and her typically developing peers were running circles around her physically and intellectually. It was like a bad accident; I didn't want to look and at the same time I couldn't look away.

As we were driving home from the picnic, I told Will, "We are NEVER hanging out with those people again. That was way too depressing!"

Two years later, I was on the board of directors for that very same Down syndrome society.

You know how when you're working out and you hate an exercise and you really want to stop but that's how you know it's exactly what you need to be doing? That's how it felt in those early days. It was painful and uncomfortable to meet people who had Down syndrome, but we kept showing up because we knew it was good for us. Even though Fern was only a baby, we attended dances and performances given by people who have Down syndrome. I'd cringe at the tuneless singing and smile weakly as I watched them dance. Then I'd go home and promise myself that Fern would do better.

As with any exercise, it got easier with practice. Instead of worrying about all the things Fern would never do, I started to notice the smiles and distinct personalities of the members with Down syndrome. I saw that there were boyfriend/girlfriend relationships within the group, and I learned about the various jobs held by the adults. I started to get excited about Fern's potential, and I suddenly wanted more opportunities for everyone who has Down syndrome.

So when someone asked me to run (uncontested) for a seat on the board, I agreed. It seemed like the right thing to do. I love to network and I'm pretty good at fundraising. I thought maybe I owed it to the group to use my skillset on its behalf. However, after only a few short months, it was pretty clear that being on the board of our local society wasn't for me. I couldn't stomach the politics and, guilty as it made me feel, I resigned with a bad taste in my mouth.

Still, the question nags at me: now that I'm a mother of a kid with special needs, am I supposed to be an advocate? How involved are we, as a family, supposed to be with the local society and the greater Down syndrome community as a whole? Should I feel guilty for not attending events specially organized for people who have Down syndrome, or is it okay to stay focused on my community of friends and family? And if we don't want to be involved in the local Down syndrome society, does that make us snobs?

By definition, being an advocate means going public with my support for people who have Down syndrome, but I've come to understand that it doesn't mean I have to stand behind a podium and make a great speech. I've learned that my life is littered with opportunities to advocate on behalf of Fern and others who have Down syndrome.

Here's an example of a conversation I've had some version of at least a hundred times. In the summer of 2014, we took the kids camping in one of our favorite state parks. Just as were finishing dinner on our first evening there, a woman with five teenagers set up camp next to us. Over the next three days, our mutual admiration and curiosity blossomed. At some point, she hollered over to us, "You're very brave for camping with all those babies!" to which Will replied, "We were thinking the same thing about you!"

Later, I ran into the woman on the way to the restroom and asked her, "So what's the story? Why are there so many kids and only one you? Do you have twins?"

She said, "They are all mine. And yes! There's a set of twins, but they look nothing alike. How about you, how old are your kids?"

I told her, "The oldest is two and a half and the twins just turned one."

She was dumbstruck. "They're twins? Gosh, they seem so different!" I knew she was referring to the fact that Fern sat planted wherever we plopped her down, while Sylvan was walking and climbing onto the picnic table.

I explained, "Well, yeah, our little girl has Down syndrome so she's not crawling yet."

She got that sad look on her face, so I saved her the trouble of figuring out what to say by redirecting the conversation. "So do you guys go camping often? Because it seems like your kids know what they're doing."

"Well, this is our third time. I waited until they were old enough to be helpful. You'll see. The twin thing has so many ups and downs. The first year is a blur, but you're headed for a downhill."

I thought she was trying to say that, given how hard the first year was, things would be all easier from here, but then I realized she was actually trying to tell me things were going to get worse. "What do you mean, downhill?"

"Well, I remember when they were a year-old and it seemed like it was getting easier. Then they both started to walk. I was chasing them every which way," Even as the words came out of her mouth it occurred to her that we already established that Fern is not walking. She stuttered a little, "And then they started school, and began to fight over friends…" She trailed off and it is obvious she is considering that maybe the pitfalls of having twins do not apply to us, that perhaps we are facing pitfalls far worse than those she is describing. Maybe kids who have Down syndrome don't have friends.

The weight of her assumptions made her falter, so I picked up the conversation by answering some of her unspoken questions. "Well, if there's anything good about developmental delays it's that at least I don't have two walkers right now. I don't know what I'd do with two kids like Sylvan! I'm sure you've seen him climbing on the picnic table?"

Relieved, she said, "Yes! My twins were climbers too!"

I said, "Well, Fern will be climbing soon enough. Kids with Down syndrome usually walk by the time they are two, and Fern is right on track. Hey, I gotta get back, but I'm so glad we met. It's really inspiring to see how peacefully your teenagers get along."

I don't take every opportunity to educate every person with whom I am engaged in casual conversation, but one way I am comfortable in the role of advocate is to demystify what it means to have Down syndrome. I don't mind sharing what I know about Down syndrome with perfect strangers, if only to show them that it's okay to talk about it. Instead of adding something new to the greater conversation about Down syndrome, I'm focused on starting as many small conversations as I can.

A new mom once told me, "I don't think I want to be an advocate." What she meant was that she is a private person and she didn't want to be the mom who made daily posts about her daughter on Facebook or the person to organize events for the local society. But I've come to understand is that when you have a child who has special needs, just letting others see you helping your child live their best life can be an act of advocacy. When you have a child with special needs, being a loving mother who is also *happy* is enough to turn the general public's opinion on its head.

As for attending every Down syndrome event, whether it is social or educational, I think you have to ask yourself whether your involvement is about you, or about your kid. I quickly realized that having a kid with special needs did not mean that I necessarily liked all the parents out there who also have kids with special needs. More often than not, the *only* thing I had in common with people at an event thrown by the local Down syndrome organization was that our children have an extra chromosome, and it turns out this is not sufficient for building a friendship. I am picky about who I keep company with. I like to surround myself with upbeat people doing interesting things and, like the general population as a whole, a lot of parents of kids with special needs can be jerks. Or worse: boring.

But, this isn't about me. There's also the sobering truth that Fern is going to need some life-long friends, and those people are going to come from the Down syndrome community.

When I think about it: Fern is not quite three but at play dates of mixed ages, Fern hangs best with kids younger than, and therefore developmentally on par, with her. But those kids are going to "outgrow" her, and Fern will soon need a new set of friends. When Fern is in third grade, she might have a third grade best friend. But that kid will outpace her socially and by fifth grade, they will be in completely different worlds. By high school, Fern will be dramatically different from her typically developing peers and if by some miracle she does still have a friend from elementary school, it cannot be denied that the only people who can truly understand Fern's struggles in this world will be other people with Down syndrome.

And for that reason alone, I might need to join another Down syndrome society and learn how to get along with some jerks. And maybe some boring people, too.

TWENTY-THREE

My Friend Amos

One of the roles I assumed as a board member was to organize our local Buddy Walk. The Buddy Walk is a national event aimed at building awareness and acceptance of Down syndrome. The Buddy Walk can also be structured as a fundraiser, with the proceeds benefitting both the local organization and the National Down syndrome Society. Everyone who has ever organized a Buddy Walk will tell you that it's a lot of work, and ours was no exception.

The night before the Buddy Walk, I was up late packing up my car so I'd be ready to go in the morning. Just before I went to bed, I made one last call. It was to a man I'd heard about who also had a set of boy-girl twins just a couple of months older than ours and, as in our case, the girl had Down syndrome. The family was Amish, so it didn't matter what time I called. I knew I'd get their answering machine. I left a long, rambling message, as I am prone to do. It went something like this:

Beep.

"Hi. My name is Heather House. I'm friends with the Fishers here in Penns Valley and they told me that you have a set of two-year-old twins and one of them has Down syndrome. I also have a set of two-year-old twins, and our girl has Down syndrome. I wonder if you'd be willing meet sometime. Maybe after farming slows down for the winter? We could come to you, maybe bring some dinner? I'm not Amish, but I'd just love to talk to you about how it's going."

I left my number, hung up and went to bed.

The next morning, I was at the event center long before sunrise. As the mother of three kids under the age of four, I had to ask myself, "What the heck am I doing here at this ungodly hour?" But there wasn't much time to reflect on why I had dragged myself out of bed to organize an event for people I hardly knew and a cause I hardly understood. Volunteers were starting to show up and there was work to do.

The walk was a success, but the day was long and I was tired and a little grouchy when I got home. Just before I collapsed on the couch, I pressed PLAY on the answering machine.

The lilting accent of an Amish person rang clear across the living room. "Hi Heather. This is David. Thank you for calling and leaving your message. Yes, we would very much like to meet you and your family. It is always good to share with others who can understand. You just know. So yeah, when the farming settles down here soon, let's get together. We would very much like to see you and your family. You know the drill. You know what it's like. You just … (pause) well, you just know."

And there was my answer for why I was up to catch the sunrise. No matter what our race, religion, socioeconomic status, we all crave connection and acceptance. Shared experience is at the heart of what makes life fulfilling and events like the annual Buddy Walk are a great way for people to connect.

Meeting Amos's family was an amazing experience. We finally connected on the phone and set up a time for our family to visit his family on their farm. At the end of October, we got up early and drove an hour and half to meet Amos and his family this morning. They had invited another Amish family who has a six month old boy with Down syndrome to join us.

As soon as we arrived and parked our van behind their friends' cart and horse, it felt like we were stepping into another world, as if we'd just disembarked a plane in South America, where everything was different. The language, the culture, the governing rules. And yet, once we sat down to exchange our stories, it was all exactly the same. The heartache, the guilt, the shame and, ultimately, the overcoming.

Amos' little girl was on the porch waving, very excited to see us. Of course, I don't have a photo, but I swear to you, she looked just like Fern except in a little Amish dress. Blonde hair, rosy cheeks, downsy eyes and downsy movements. The same crazy contrast of fluid, unreal movements made possible by hypotonic muscles interspersed with unsteady halted gross motor movements created by those same hypotonic muscles. I loved her instantly and she was all smiles for me. Later we will realize that everyone had made an effort to clean up for our visit, and that maybe she was cleaned up a little extra for us. Her hair was tied in a rolling braid on either side of her head, with the hair being gathered in the back and tightly wound onto itself and clipped just above the temple with folded metal strips. I asked where they got those strips, thinking they might stay in Fern's fine hair, and they proudly said they came from off the packages of saltine crackers. I couldn't believe Ana would hold still long enough for such a tidy hairdo, but a few months later during our trip to the islands, Fern would sit still as a heron while a Jamaican woman coo-ed to her and braided her hair. I believed Fern would never allow me to do such a thing, but it's probably another example of how expectation shapes behavior.

So it was me and Will and our three kids (which always seems like a lot until you visit an Amish family); Amos, his wife and their eleven children; and Amos' friends and seven children. Amish home may not have electricity, but there was a chair for every one of us and we all circled up in their living room to talk about this thing we have in common.

And honestly, it was kind of amazing.

Amos, his wife and their friends shared their experience of grief and surprise with us, and we shared our stories too. We compared notes on heart surgeries, homemade formulas, eye doctors etc. Will and I were sure we were breaking all kinds of unspoken social rules, but they tolerated our kids playing on the floor and indulged our suggestion that the desserts I'd brought be shared around. Their stories read just like mine. I kind of wondered whether they would have an "It's all in God's plan" take on things and when I asked Amos about this he said, "Well sure, but I'm still human. I've got an ego and I have to get past that to see into God's plan."

Amos wanted to know, "Did you get a lot of letters from your community?"

I shrugged, "I'm not sure what you mean."

"Oh, right. You have facebook and emails, not letters."

"Oh, I see. Actually, yes, we did get quite a few letters and lots of messages from our community via facebook and email. And we had a lot of visitors too."

"Wasn't that great? We felt really glad to get those letters, to be supported like that."

"Yes, us too. It was a relief."

Amos asked, "How do you mean, relief?"

"Well, I was worried that people would drop us, that they would reject us now that we had a kid with special needs. I was relieved when people did the opposite and actually embraced us."

"I see. I wouldn't say it was a relief for us, because we knew the community would be there. But it was unexpected, the kindness. It meant a lot to receive so many letters."

I admired how they allowed their children to listen to them process this incredible thing, to share their grief and their triumphs so openly. The older kids were maybe 20 and the youngest still spoke only Pennsylvania Dutch, and yet there they were all listening respectfully. No one lowered their voice to whisper about the horror of seeing their child after heart surgery, no one tried to cover up the crisis of identity and how we were coming through it. It seemed to me a very healthy approach, to allow our kids to see our vulnerabilities and to let them be a part of the process of healing.

We came away from that meeting humbled by the knowledge that there are a lot of ways to raise a kid who has Down syndrome. It's not just about meeting milestones or following a rule book. In a culture that so heavily depends on the participation of everyone, there's a way that Fern's friend will benefit from being given responsibilities that most kids with Down syndrome will never have, such as handling milking cows and gathering eggs. We wondered too at their plan to isolate their little girl in a small preschool with only two students rather than integrate her into the one room school house, but knew for certain it was not our place to judge.

Perhaps the most poignant moment for me was when we all acknowledged that it took us a little extra effort to love our kids with Down syndrome, to include them, to do more than just care for them. We made our guilty confessions and we noted how there's a difference between tolerating a child's presence in your life or experiencing acceptance of your fate, and truly loving a child. I made the choice to love Fern a long time ago, but I remember how ashamed I felt that I was even having to make that choice. And loving Fern, while lovely, is not enough. I want to need Fern the way I need oxygen. My new friends? They understood this perfectly.

TWENTY-FOUR

Hurry up, Nestra

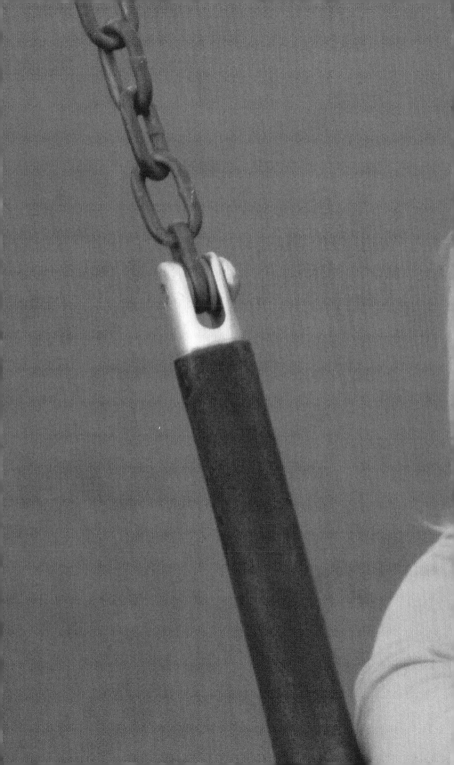

It appears that my desire for Fern to one day have a job may be at odds with my desire to get out of the supermarket as quickly as possible.

I realized this on Wednesday night when I pushed my cart to stand behind the stout man in aisle 4. He didn't have a cart, so I assumed the wait would be short. Then I noticed he was also empty handed.

"Excuse me," I asked. "Are you in line?"

"Yeah," he said, gesturing with a thumb. "My wife is coming with the cart now." He turned to face me. "The cashier over there is *really* slow." Emphasis on the 'really.'

Just then his doughy wife toddled over with a very full cart, an 'excuse me but that's my place in line' smile on her face. I maneuvered my cart to make room for her.

"I mean," the man continued with no prompting from me, "the cashier was *really slow*." I understood that he was hinting at something and, in doing so, inviting me to join him in banter. But I was too distracted by the fullness of their cart to pay much attention. I wanted a shorter line.

The man unloaded his cart while his wife dug for something in her purse. "Let's hope this guy is moving at normal speed," the man said. "Because that other one...sheez!" He was trying to catch my attention, clearly wanting to vent.

Then it dawned on me what he was saying: the cashier was mentally challenged.

The next aisle looked promising. I disengaged myself by saying, "Yeah. Let's hope so," and turned away.

I pulled, rather than pushed, the nose of my cart into line, which put a wall of magazines and gum between me and the stout man with his doughy wife. I turned my attention to emptying the contents of my cart onto the conveyor, and stewed.

So what. The cashier is mentally challenged. They need jobs too. That could be my daughter Fern one day. What's your freaking hurry anyway, dude?

The cashier in my aisle handed a receipt to the customer two places ahead of me, then he turned to the middle aged couple standing next in line. He greeted them with a big smile and began sliding their items across the scanner. They had, at most, fifteen small items and one big Tonka truck.

The couple made friendly small talk with me and within the span of a minute I learned that it was the man's 60th birthday. I joked that perhaps the Tonka truck was for his birthday.

"No," the wife laughed. "We're getting this for our grandson." Then her eyes widened and she smiled at something over my shoulder. "Oh! There's a baby on your back!" It was my son Sylvan, who waved from his perch in his sling.

Sylvan is usually content to ride on my back for the duration of a shopping trip, but on this night he was getting restless. It was 45 minutes past bedtime and he was letting me know that it was time to go home by arching backwards in an effort to get out of the sling. With each straining of his body he made a grunting noise that sounded like a trapped seal. Since we were next in line, I decided the best thing might be for Sylvan to get down and stretch his legs for the few minutes it would take to check out. I untied the carrier and reached under Sylvan's arms to bring him around to the ground in front of me. Meltdown avoided, for the moment.

The sound of my internal mommy clock went tick tick tick tick tick. We had about seven minutes before Sylvan would explode. All I had to do was keep him engaged while the cashier finished up with the couple in front of me, then I could get Sylvan's "help" bagging the groceries. That might buy us a little more time, hopefully enough to get everything loaded and out the door where Will would be waiting for us with the van.

That's when I noticed how interminably slow our cashier was moving. According to the name tag pinned to his blue cashiers'vest, his name was Nestra. He appeared to be about 25 years old, perhaps from Nepal or Northern India judging from his lustrous dark hair, deep black eyes and skin the color of weak tea. And from the lack of stickers, pins and pithy statements about his number of years in service on his name badge, I guessed he was also new on the job.

Ah, yes. There is a woman in a matching blue vest standing at his shoulder. That must be his trainer. Lucky me.

I have a reputation for being quick to a fault. Even when I'm doing yoga I can be a bit of a pistol. It pains me to witness inefficiency, and watching Nestra move like cold molasses was triggering a stress response in my body. My pulse quicken, my jaw tightened and my knees started to lock up.

So slowly did Nestra reach for a bag of frozen carrots on the conveyor, I had to restrain myself from reaching out to hand them to him to speed things up. As he dragged the plastic bag across the scanner I prayed, *Please God, let the scanner read the UPC code.* And when the scanner did not pick up the code, I cursed inwardly and proceeded to hold my breath while I strained to hear the confirmation of the "beep" as Nestra dragged the bag across the scanner again. And then once more.

Beep.

Phew.

But now Nestra had a new challenge: which bag should the frozen carrots go in?

Nestra turned to his trainer. "Do we put frozen goods with canned goods?"

"I like to keep frozen goods separate from everything else," the trainer answered.

There was a lull in the action. Nestra held the bag of frozen carrots in one hand, poised to pack, while he swiped at the neck of a new plastic bag, trying to gain enough traction to pry it open.

I willed the couple in front of me to take the items from Nestra's uncertain hands and bag for themselves. But they busied themselves planning for the upcoming party for their grandson.

Watching Nestra was killing me. I needed a distraction, so I squatted to focus on Sylvan, who was eager to touch all the colorful goodies lined-up for impulse purchasing.

His hand reached out. "No no. Don't touch," I said. And he listened, pulling his hand away from the candy placed perfectly at his eye-level.

Then his little dimpled hand reached out again. "No no. Don't touch," I said. And, again, he listened, pulling his hand away from the batteries that hung a bit lower.

After a moment, his little hand went out again. It didn't seem fair to taunt him with all the things he couldn't touch, so I picked him up.

Oh dear. The trainer stood just over Nestra's shoulder pointing at the computer screen. *The couple has a coupon.*

Sylvan squirmed as Nestra wrapped up the couple's transaction.

Then Nestra turned to me and made eye contact. "Good evening!" he said cheerfully as he reached for my first item.

I smiled. How nice to be greeted with such earnestness! He was genuinely a nice person. That must have helped him land the job.

"How are you?" I said, returning his smile.

And Nestra, being a person who cannot talk and move at the same time, paused to answer, "Fine, thank you."

"Great," I said, switching to a cooler tone and shifting my attention to Sylvan. No way were we going to have a conversation if Nestra couldn't keep moving. Will was probably waiting for us outside now and my mommy clock told me we were officially on borrowed time. I put Sylvan in the empty cart where he could admire our groceries as they slid past him.

Nestra scanned our first item, a can of beans.

Beep.

Sylvan grabbed an avocado and tossed it to the ground. The lady in line behind us picked it up and I noticed her for the first time. She had a really pretty face and beautifully styled blonde hair, and enormous thighs crammed into extremely tight jeans. I shot her a grateful smile.

Nestra picked up our second item, a block of cheese.

Beep.

Then Nestra debated whether to put the cheese in the same bag as the canned beans. Cheese is not frozen, but it's cold and that must have been what threw him.

Sylvan tossed another avocado to the ground. The lady behind us picked it up. I noticed her cart contained was laden with ten cases of diet soda. I said, "I'm sorry. Thanks."

As Nestra reached for our third item, I picked up Sylvan. And, seeing that he was going to be restrained from throwing more food on the ground, Sylvan began to wail.

Beep.

I adjusted the carrier and returned Sylvan to his perch on my back. As I cinched his body close to mine, I turned to the lady in line behind me and joked, "This way he can scream directly into my ear, ha ha." Which is precisely what he did.

Beep.

I bounced up and down, swished my butt back and forth, and rocked heel-toe, heel-toe. Still, Sylvan wailed in protest. He arched his back so that his head was only millimeters from hitting the gum rack behind me, then he flailed himself forward, slamming his chest between my shoulder blades and burying his face in my neck. From the corner of my eye, I could see he was red-faced.

At that moment, I noticed the stout man and his doughy wife wheeling past me on their way out the door. It seemed impossible that they were already leaving. They had at least three times the number of items in their cart as me. They looked at me sideways, probably wondering how I planned to get my kid under control.

I reached for the bagels on the conveyor. "Please ring these up next so I can give one to my baby."

Nestra looked at me with dark uncomprehending eyes. Perhaps English was not his first language. I softened a little.

"The bagels," I said over Sylvan's screams. "Ring them up please."

Nesta ran them across the scanner.

No beep.

He tried again.

No beep.

The trainer reached over to show him how to flatten the plastic so that the UPC code could be read by the scanner.

Beep.

I snatched the bag from Nestra, tore off the plastic closure and handed Sylvan a bagel. He gripped it tightly without even the slightest break in his screams.

I patted. I shhhhhed. I sang and pleaded.

The lady in line behind me looked distressed, and the way her eyes darted about I guessed she was formulating an exit strategy. She was displeased, and she wanted me to know it.

For crap's sake! I'm doing the best I can, lady! Just leave if this is too much for you. Kids cry. Get over it.

Sylvan was inconsolable. I rummaged through my purse for something to give him, but it was too late. All he wanted was to go to bed.

What now? I noticed that Nestra and his trainer were studying the produce chart.

"What is this?" they asked.

"It's a kabocha pumpkin." I answered. "They are 88 cents a pound."

The trainer and Nestra continued to study the chart.

"It's a kind of pumpkin," I said helpfully over Sylvan's yowls.

They flipped the chart over, presumably to look under "p."

Sylvan's screams went up an octave.

Fuck the kabocha.

"Forget the pumpkin," I said. The trainer and Nestra looked confused.

"You don't want the pumpkin?" Nestra asked.

"No, thanks," I said, fake smile plastered to my face. *Perhaps you haven't noticed, but my kid is screaming and everyone in this store hates me. I just want to get the hell out of here.*

Nestra looked dazed and I swear I could read his mind. "Hmmmm, what to do with a pumpkin the lady doesn't want to buy?" The trainer must have had a customer meltdown clock that she alone could hear *(tick tick tick tick)* because she grabbed the kabocha from Nestra and tucked it under the counter.

Nestra gathered himself. He actually took a breath and wiped his hands on his apron as if readying to face another round of hard ball. Then he reached for the next item.

Beep.

Beep.

Silence.

Now what???

Nestra was debating whether the bruised avocadoes could go with the bananas.

I had had enough.

"Nestra!" I said, using his name for effect. I snapped my fingers. "You gotta pick up the pace, buddy!" Nestra gave me a slow blink. My tone was friendly and I was smiling, but it was clear that I meant what I said. His trainer gave me a funny look. Was she thinking, "OMG crazy bitch alert!" Or was it possible she was thinking, "Wish I had said that." Either way, to my amazement, Nestra sped up.

Beep, beep, beep, beep.

The price of picking up the pace meant there was no rhyme or reason to his bagging. The trainer opened the plastic bags for him and Nestra, intent on moving a little quicker, placed just one item per bag.

Sylvan's tantrum had plateaued and he was losing steam. Now he just whimpered and whined and kicked his little legs against my hips.

Finally. The total.

"Do you want cash back?" Nestra asked.

"No thanks." *I do not want anything that could possibly complicate this transaction any further. It took me 20 minutes to do the grocery shopping and 18 minutes to check out. In fact, I no longer feel guilty about forgetting my cloth bags. I can only imagine how that might have thrown you!*

Receipt in hand, I bid Nestra and his trainer good night and headed for the door. As I walked, Sylvan grew quiet. By the time we stood in our designated meeting place in front of the store, Sylvan munched contentedly on his bagel. A chilly wind whistled through our many, many plastic bags. While we waited for Will, I took a minute to reflect on what had just happened.

Fern has Down syndrome and, in being Fern's mom, I've released much of my need for life to go a certain way. Yet, I still sweat so much of the small stuff. It's as if I can more easily release big dreams, like that of raising a daughter who will go to Harvard and bring her children to visit their grandmother on holidays, than I can accept that we may be a few minutes late meeting up with Will because our cashier is slow. I often feel caught in the eddy at the confluence of serenity and outrage, with my loyalty to Fern being the only thing that keeps me from crashing on the jagged rocks of my hot tempered judgment below.

And oh do I weld my double standard like a switch! I lash out with my judging bad thoughts against anyone who suggests there is not a place for people with special needs in our world, and simultaneously whip into action someone who doesn't meet my personal need for efficiency. I want to believe that something fundamental has shifted in me and that I am now more accepting of all kinds of people in the world. Yet, at the first sign the woman standing in line behind me, who I practically gave myself an award for noticing had a pretty face and a nice hairdo, was feeling irritated with my unruly son, I turned and use the shallow observations I made about her thighs and soda purchase to mentally slice her at the knees.

The descent from riding my high white horse into Nestra's aisle 3, feeling both protective of people who have special needs and annoyed that people aren't more accepting of each other, to wallowing in the most deplorable of thoughts, ("For God's sake, Nestra! At least my kid has a diagnosis!"), took all of about three minutes.

Once, just weeks after Fern was born, we met a man whose passion it was to help people with special needs get jobs. I understood this to be his "volunteer" work, having otherwise made a great deal of money doing something that required nice clothes and a good haircut. Will and I were still walking around in a daze, trying to figure out what Fern's diagnosis meant for all of us. This man, a gentleman in all respects, assured us that the prospects of Fern having a job one day were good. He said, "I just placed two people with Down syndrome on the cleanup crew at Taco Bell." I know he thought he was being helpful, but I didn't find the thought comforting. It wasn't just my prejudice against fast food joints. I simply failed to see the connection between living a fulfilling life and having a job. Lord knows I have had plenty of "good jobs." At just six weeks old, I wasn't worried about whether or not Fern would have a job. Instead, I was still wondering whether she was going to fit in, be loved and accepted for who she was. I wasn't ready to pin my hopes on Fern being able to push a mop around a fast food joint.

I surprised myself by responding with a discourteous tone. "That's nice," I said, "But you can imagine I want something more for my daughter." He readily agreed and the conversation came to abrupt halt. As we walked away, I mumbled to Will that there may very well come a day when we celebrate Fern landing a job on the cleaning crew at a fast food restaurant. "But it sure as hell ain't gonna be Taco Bell."

The more people I meet who have Down syndrome, the more I understand that working as a cashier would actually be quite a feather in Fern's cap. Cashiering requires only a few very basic skills, skills that I hope Fern will master someday. But what distinguishes a functioning cashier from a great one is speed, a penchant for a little friendly small talk without interrupting the task at hand, and the ability to pack like a nest-building warbler. Fern probably won't have what it takes to be a *great* cashier.

No matter what her job turns out to be, poor fine motor skills, the need for more time to process information, and slower response times might make Fern the perfect target for hot tempered people like her mama. And this worries me.

In a perverse interpretation of karma, this Mama Bear feels as though every time I fail to be fully present with someone who could use a little extra time, like Nestra, I have made a withdrawal from our collective reserve of patience. And every time I take a mental jab at people who have, essentially, done nothing to harm me, I have missed an opportunity to make a deposit into our collective reserve of kindness. Will there be a shortfall at some critical time in the future when my own Baby Bear needs a bit of compassion from a stranger?

As I stood outside of the store that guarantees the lowest prices (but not the fastest service), I felt ashamed of myself. Although Fern's diagnosis shattered any illusions I harbored that I have control over the events in my life, I seemed to have dodged a bullet when it comes to being a better person. Instead of using the experience of having a child with special needs to become a more compassionate person, (an outcome many mothers of children with special needs promised me), I only seem to be developing a heighted awareness of all the times that I fail to be my best self.

I used to laugh ruefully at myself when I fell short of being the person I want to be, chucking it up to one of life's experiences, just another opportunity for growth lost to an impulsive reaction. Now, with Fern in my life, when I fail to be compassionate, or patient, or simply kind, I feel genuine shame. I am ashamed that the thoughts I have about certain people could cause them pain. I am ashamed that I can't seem to live a little softer in a world that has plenty of sharp edges. And I am ashamed of how I fail the sorority of motherhood when I criticize another woman's child. Mothers of the world, me and Nestra's mother included, do not wish to be made to defend their children's perceived weaknesses. Our shared hope is that the world will welcome our children and celebrate their gifts, regardless of whether they are the fastest, smartest, thinnest or prettiest of them all.

TWENTY-FIVE

Down Syndrome for Sale

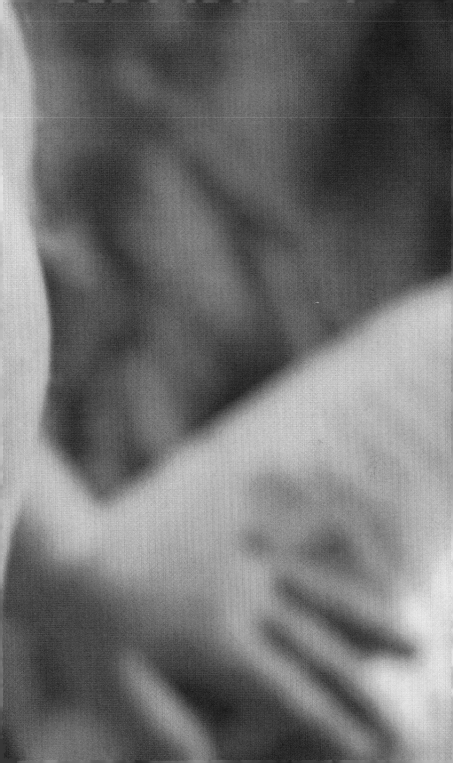

This Amish lady walked up to our family at the farmer's market and said, "Are those twins?" pointing at Sylvan, who was in my arms, and Fern, who was being held by Will.

"Yes, they are," I said. "And this is their big brother, Cypress. He just turned two," making a point to include Cypress at a time when so much attention was given to his siblings.

The Amish woman looked admiringly at Sylvan, and then took a closer look at Fern. "But she is so much smaller than him!"

"Yes," Will answered, not bothering to add any of the colorful details that explained Fern's size, like her low birth weight and the hole in her heart. At five months old, Fern was barely half the size of her twin.

The Amish woman asked in her lilting English, "So does she have Down syndrome?"

"Yes," Will answered, again adding nothing.

"Well, can I hold her?" the Amish woman asked, practically scooping Fern out of Will's arms before he had a chance to answer with another, "Yes."

People often approached us to ask about our twins. They commented on the babies' matching blonde fuzzy heads, and their startling blue eyes, Fern's being the deep blue shade of a churning ocean and Sylvan's the color of a clear spring sky. They commented on the size difference, Fern being tiny for their age and Sylvan being long. And, always, they said, "Well, you sure do have your hands full!"

But until this moment, no one had ever said, "Does she have Down syndrome?" I constantly wondered whether it was obvious to strangers that Fern had Down syndrome. Hell, I thought about it so often I even wondered whether our dog Ko Ko could tell. The way she cautiously sniffed Fern's head seemed suspicious to me. But no one had ever said anything and it had gotten so that I almost believed my husband when he said that Down syndrome wasn't the first thing people noticed about Fern. It was not until the twins were five months old that a total stranger, the Amish woman at the farmers' market, openly acknowledged that Fern looked different or, more specifically, that she looked like she had Down syndrome. And the experience, for me, was profound.

It was a relief to know what the other person was thinking. When the Amish woman scooped up Fern like she couldn't wait to get her hands on her, I had to walk away to hide my tears. She could have asked to hold Sylvan, but she chose Fern. Not because she pitied Fern, but because she found Fern irresistible. Until this woman poured her affection on my child who she knew had special needs, I didn't know this reaction was possible from a stranger.

The older Fern gets, the more obvious her tell-tale characteristics of Down syndrome become. She is pretty, with rosy cheeks and bright blonde hair. Strangers ooooh and aaaaah over her when they first meet her. But give it a second, and you can see they are trying to puzzle it out for themselves.

Something in the way Fern's reaction time is a little slower, the way her eyes are a little duller, the way her movements are a little less purposeful, the way her mouth hangs open when she looks at you uncomprehendingly. She's different. Whether it is social covenants or lack of curiosity, no one ever asks about it. And the "not asking" has become a little uncomfortable for me, especially when I can see the other person has questions.

In stark contrast to Will, who never feels compelled to explain to anyone that Fern has Down syndrome, I kind of amaze myself with new and creative ways for working Fern's diagnosis into a conversation. If it is an art-form, then I am a master.

A friend might mention they are hung over because they were out celebrating their 21st birthday and I'll say, "Oh! What a coincidence! My daughter Fern has an extra 21st chromosome!"

Or someone might comment, "That's such a pretty dress!" and I'll say, "You think so? I wasn't sure how it would go with the extra chromosome."

To avoid the uncomfortable questioning, but not-asking, silence of strangers, I often just volunteer the information. Here's a typical conversation:

A stranger approaches and asks, "Are they twins?"

I say, "Yes, they are."

"Are they identical?"

"No, ones a boy and ones a girl."

"Oh! Which one is the girl?"

"The one wearing pink," I say, pointing to Fern. "She also has Down syndrome."

Maybe I'm jumping the gun. Certainly, people don't always know what to do with my forthrightness. And maybe I am the odd bird because I don't consider matters of my daughter's diagnosis to be private in nature. Being forthright is my way of combatting ignorance, and combatting ignorance is my way of advocating.

But let us go back to the beginning of the story, to the moment when the Amish woman approached me and my family at market. I want to take a minute to reflect, not on the details of the story, but on the telling of it. After I shared the story of the Amish woman on Facebook, I began to wonder why I had to include the fact that the lady in the story was Amish at all, since that had nothing to do with the point of the story. I would have been as moved by her direct inquiry and obvious affection had the woman been Jewish, or black, or a man. The moral of the story wasn't, "Amish people sometimes surprise you," but rather, "It was a relief to know that people can see that Fern has Down syndrome and still be drawn to her."

It bothered me that I let one small descriptor, "Amish," sum up the character of this woman. I could have mentioned that this woman had an easy way about her, something honest and warm that made it easy for Will to hand our baby over to her. I could have said that even though she was wearing glasses I could still see past the glare on the lens to the kindness in her eyes. I didn't mention any of this, only that she was Amish.

And I knew exactly why: the first thing you notice about an Amish person is that they are Amish. Their distinct plain clothes, haircuts, aprons, suspenders and stockings all say, "Amish." Just as Fern's almond-shaped eyes, flat bridge of the nose and lower set ears all say, "Down syndrome."

But do I want all the stories people tell about Fern to begin, "This girl with Down syndrome..."? Do I want everything Fern does to be qualified by her diagnosis?

Don't get me wrong. I want you to talk about my daughter. I *need* you to talk about Fern and Down syndrome and all the great things you see her doing. Silence only perpetuates myths and misunderstandings. What I'm hoping, though, is that when stories begin, "This kid with Down syndrome....," as they sometimes will, we consider what we are trying to imply. Are we saying, "Given our obvious low expectations of this person because of their disability, this story is surprising?" Or "Isn't this story just typical of people who have disabilities?" Are we to understand that the protagonist in your story is slow? Different looking? Not very smart? When does adding "Down syndrome" as a qualifier add to the story?

When I started my professional career in the agriculture-based non-profit world, one of my first duties was to update a brochure about locally available farm products. Having completed the first draft, I took the brochure around to the farmers at the local market for their approval. The brochure contained descriptions of the products and the farmers who made them. When I showed the brochure to a man named Eli, who was Amish, he took exception to the paragraph dedicated to his stand, which described his products as "Amish baked goods." He told me, "You forgot to label the Catholic-grown carrots and Baptist canned goods. Why not just say I sell Shoo Fly Pie?"

Eli had a point, though using "Amish-made" as a marketing point was hardly my unique idea. In fact, in Central Pennsylvania, you see signs touting "Amish-made" products everywhere; usually the claim is made by English people retailing Amish products but every now and then an Amish person will set out a simple white sign with black lettering that reads "Amish-made." Because everyone knows a hand-painted Amish sign when they see it, it's a little redundant to state "Amish-made," but maybe they don't want to miss an opportunity to cash in on their collective reputation for making quality goods,

Now that I have Fern, I understand more fully what Eli was saying, and this cashing-in on an identity is starting to irk me.

When I asked Will whether it was okay for a business to brag about hiring people with special needs he said, "Hell yes! They are creating an opportunity not only for the person with special needs, but for every person that comes into contact with them. Plus it makes other businesses want to hire people with special needs."

But I'm not so sure. "But I wonder if in celebrating the businesses that hire people with special needs we are inadvertently reinforcing the idea that hiring people with special needs is, in fact, an exception to how the regular workplace functions?"

"You're saying that people like Fern should just be expected to work like anyone else?"

"Well, yes. I don't want someone to hire Fern just because she has special needs. I want them to hire her because she can get the job done."

"I think you are too idealistic."

"But it is the idealism of parents before us that has gotten us to where we are, Will. Fifty years ago, it was considered unrealistic to take a baby with special needs home from the hospital instead of institutionalizing them."

He is thoughtful. "Maybe, but if someone is making an extra effort to hire my daughter, then I think they deserve kudos."

"And what if they are only hiring Fern to check 'be socially just' off their list? Like they are using her so they can brag about it?"

"So what! The outcome is the same. Fern has a job and people get to see a person with special needs work. And that exposure is priceless." Will has experience working with a crew of janitors from a job placement service for people who have special needs. "I saw them do work that no one else wanted to do. And they did it joyously!"

"I'm not saying Fern has to be hired as CEO. I don't care if she's a janitor, so long as she is as good a janitor as any typically developed person. But I'm not sure it's right for her employer to capitalize on her disability."

"And I think that it's too early to split those hairs."

"This feels a little like affirmative action."

"What do you mean by that?" asked Will.

"I mean, black people were underrepresented in the workforce for years. Affirmative action meant more people of color were given the opportunity to prove themselves in the workplace. But I think everyone would agree that while the color of one's skin might have influenced the hiring decision, it is up to the individual to do the job well."

"Okay, and...?"

"Well, maybe we need something like Affirmative Action to help Fern get a foot in the door. Maybe that help will come from a workplace that prides itself on being inclusive, but it will be up to her to be a good worker. I want believe that, for certain jobs, Fern could be competitive in the workplace. I want Fern to be hired and retained as an employee because she is contributing to the workforce and earning her wage by being a good employee."

"I think you have a very narrow definition of what it means to contribute. Just by being herself and by interacting with other people, Fern will be contributing. She will help people be more compassionate. She helps people see outside of themselves."

"Hmph," I smiled. "Now who's being idealistic?"

"Seriously, Heather. There's more to being a good employee than working hard. What Fern contributes is intangible. Until you meet her and are changed by her. And then, what Fern brings to the table is invaluable."

"Okay. I see that," I said. "Still, I think we are working towards holding it as common knowledge that our kids should be treated like just another employee who is making a meaningful contribution to the workforce in exchange for fair pay."

"It sounds like you are being very black and white about this," replied Will.

"I'm not trying to be. I'm just thinking out loud. Do we celebrate businesses for hiring kids like Fern, or do we ask them to not use our kids as poster children for their own gain?"

It's complicated. Marketing, the practice of creating and cashing in on an identity, can be as educational as it is opportunistic. On the one hand, I understand that consumers may be more willing to purchase a product, perhaps even pay a little more for it, if they know the story behind the product or business. This is especially true if the consumer believes the business or product to be made in a way that is "socially just."

If a business creates jobs for individuals who might otherwise not find employment, and they brag on it a little to generate a sale, that's just good marketing, right? But I wonder...when a label says, "Made by People with Disabilities," what is the collective identity we are hoping to cash in on? Are we saying, "Support a business that employs people who otherwise don't have work?" Are we educating the general public that a disabled population can work? Or is it the label really so the business can say, "Hey! Look at us! We're soft hearted and trying to do the right thing?"

Marketing can also be emotional blackmail, and that's where the line gets blurry for me. I recently had a mini-crisis at an arts festival where I had a little cash to treat myself to something nice. I had my eye on a remarkable silver pendant in the shape of a ginko flower, but right next to that jeweler were some lovely soaps, made by people who have special needs. I hated the conflict within me. Just because I have a kid with special needs, do I now have to support all things special needs? Can't I just buy the pendant, which was made by a local artisan? Isn't it enough to support a local artisan? Why does everything have to have an angle anyway? In the end, I bought nothing.

Using the social justice angle might make the first sale, but only a good product at a fair price will generate repeat sales. I never want anyone to purchase something from Fern, or her employer, because they feel sorry for her. I want Fern to know that if she is going to sell something, she has to use more than her disability to make the sale.

The reality is that the opportunities Fern will have in 20 years are being shaped by events happening in the workplace right now. This is why I'm kind of obsessed with meeting working adults who have Down syndrome. I just met a man named James who, when I asked him what he did for his job at the placement agency, said, "I do boxes and bottles." I'm not sure what that meant but he was very proud. It was really interesting to hear him talk about his work and also about getting paid for certain parts of his job and not being paid for other parts. He was with his girlfriend Louise, who was adamant he needed to quit his job and try to "get into pushing carts" to "advance his career." Those were her words, "advance your career." At first I thought it was kind of hilarious how she thought if he got into picking up carts from the grocery store parking would really "advance his career." But later when I reflected on the conversation I realized that I had better stop laughing and get serious about helping James advance his career. Because maybe he's not heading for CEO, but if pushing carts is a realistic career advancement, then someone needs to help him do that.

I often tell Will that we are part of great social experiment and the results are unfolding before our very eyes. I don't have the answers about how I want you to talk about my daughter, and I don't know how I feel about using her disability to market a product, because the answer is evolving. The key is to allow this language to develop without getting bent out of shape when it changes. Just a few decades ago people like Fern were institutionalized. Now, I'm worried that her future employer might want to capitalize on her disability. Maybe it is a good problem to have.

TWENTY-SIX

Parenting Fern

Not many moms allow their toddlers, whether they have Down syndrome or not, the freedom to walk in the grocery store, and I was pleased by the look of joy on Fern's face when I lifted her out of the cart and set her on the floor. Just shy of two years old and she had *finally* learned to walk. Another of those hard-won milestones had been met, and I thought we should celebrate with a little taste of freedom. We were on an all-too-rare mother-daughter outing to get some groceries and, since it was just the two of us, I offered her the same opportunity I'd given the boys when they first learned to walk: the liberty to explore the aisle while I shopped. For them, it's a taste of independence and the sense of responsibility that comes with it was right on the growing edge for Fern, and she was heady with it.

Almost immediately, Fern headed for the glass jars on the bottom shelf.

"Ehn!" I made my signature barking noise. I use it for all my kids, but it's particularly effective with Fern. It got her attention and she froze mid-reach.

"Don't touch," I said, using the accompanying sign language we'd been working on.

Fern backed away.

Whoever says having a dog is nothing like having children is lying. Will and I adopted a rescue dog named Ko Ko long before we became parents, and we feel that co-parenting Ko Ko was pretty good practice for co-parenting human beings. When you take a dog to obedience school, it's not really the dog they're training. It's you, the owner. They don't teach the dog how to sit. They teach you, the owner, how to convey to the dog that you expect it to sit. Further, they empower you with the authority to enforce this expectation by pointing out you've got the opposable thumbs that can open the treat bag.

To me, kids are a lot like dogs, constantly asking with their actions, "Who's in charge here?" And, in my experience, they want the answer to be, "Me, your parent. I'm in charge and I'm a capable leader who loves and wants the best for you."

So there we were in the grocery store, Fern asking, "Who's in charge?" and "Can I do this?" She stepped back from the glass jars and made a bee-line for the rice bags, blonde wispy pigtails bouncing a little as she toddled.

"Ehn!" I said, again making the chopping sign with my hands. "Let's not touch. Just walk."

Fern backed away. I knew she understood. We had been told that Fern probably wouldn't walk until she was two, but we had to figure out for ourselves that gross motor milestones weren't always the best indicators of what she was capable of understanding or doing. Fern may have taken a full year longer than her twin brother to learn to walk, but cognitively she was only lagging behind him by a few months. Though the cognitive gap between Fern and her typically developing twin was widening, and the divide would only get greater as time went on, the commands, "don't touch," "don't pull hair" and "keep your plate on the table," were concepts Fern understood perfectly. That day, she just needed help connecting that "Don't touch" meant the same thing in the grocery store as it did at home.

After a moment's hesitation, she went back to the jars. Okay, I could see that one coming.

One of my heroes is the inspirational farmer/author Joel Salatin, who argues that the best way to manage a healthy, clean, profitable farm is to provide an environment where a pig can express its piggy-ness, a cow can express its cow-iness, and a chicken can express its chicken-iness. That's kind of how I parent. I want Fern to be the best Fern she can be. I'm not thinking in terms of how to "normalize" her or help her "fit in." Instead, I am looking for ways to express her Fern-iness, even if it's quirky and delayed, and even if it sometimes makes people uncomfortable.

The purpose of letting her walk the grocery aisle is not to set her up to fail. I want her to experience freedom, to know that I trust her, to learn that she can trust herself. It is a chance for Fern to express some of her Fern-iness while showing me she can listen and respond.

"Ehn," I said, a little more urgently. No gestures required. Satisfied I meant business, Fern seemed content to walk back and forth, stitching the sides of the aisle together with her footsteps while I grabbed a couple of cans of coconut milk.

We were both amazed and entertained by her hard-earned walking freedom. Waiting for Fern to walk had been difficult, especially when her twin, Sylvan, was a born athlete. Once, when Sylvan didn't know I was watching, I saw him test his standing legs and give himself a self-satisfied smile. It was only a matter of time before he would walk and I was both excited and sad. I thought, "Why do you have to grow up so fast?" Paradoxically, just second later, I looked at Fern still propped with towels in her Bumbo and I felt a wave of impatience. "Come on, Fern!" I mentally wailed, "Can't you grow any faster?"

Now, there she was, practicing the art of changing direction mid-step, wearing a clean matching dress-and-knickers set and cute teal patterned shoes I'd handmade for her. I will let the boys go out looking like ragamuffins, with holes in their pants and their hair in a tangle of knots and yard debris, but I am not nearly so casual with Fern. Before we go out, she gets a clean dress and I run a brush through her hair. When people take a little longer to look at Fern, I want them to know she is cared for and loved. Maybe this double standard in parenting is because I find it irritating to see a well-dressed family out and about with their disabled family member dressed in a baggy t-shirt and ill-fitting jeans. Or maybe it's because Fern is my girl.

I started pushing the cart down the aisle and said, "Okay, Fern. Let's go! Come with mama."

Fern walked in the opposite direction.

People often ask me if parenting Fern is any different from parenting her brothers. I'm probably supposed to answer with something like, "No, I plan to raise Fern just like my other children." Or, "We have high expectations for all of our children."

Let's just cut to the chase: everything, and I mean *everything*, I do and think about when it comes to parenting Fern passes through the "Fern-Has-Down-syndrome" filter.

On the ride to the grocery store, Fern sat in the middle row of our minivan and, on this particular day, her brother's car seats sat empty in the "way back." I like to have Fern within arm's reach, not because she can't handle sitting in the way back but because I love giving her thighs a little squeeze every now and then. Besides, I never want anyone to think she's back there behind all of us because she is the one with the disability. Just as we pulled into the grocery store parking lot, I caught her eye in the rear view mirror. She smiled at me. Then she crossed her eyes, stuck out her tongue and blew a loud happy, "Pthbthbthbthbthbtttt!" When she does this, she looks, well... dumb. And it bothers me. It does not bother me a bit when her brothers do it, but they don't have Down syndrome, and no one assumes they are dumb. Alas, it was just me and her, (and there was nothing to be done about it anyway), so I stuck out my tongue and "pthbthbthtttt!" right back at her. A shared fit of giggles was my reward.

But now, standing in the international section on aisle eight of our favorite grocery store, I was not laughing. It was irritating that Fern was heading in the opposite direction. It was all part of the learning and her brothers did the same thing on their first walk of freedom, and it was no less irritating then either. The difference was that where I was certain the boys were purposefully ignoring me, I had to figure out whether Fern had understood the command. I was pretty sure she understood "come" and I knew for certain she understood "mama." If she was putting the concepts together, then walking away was an act of defiance, perfectly "normal" for a two-year-old. But if she didn't know what I was asking of her, or for some reason wasn't able to concentrate enough while walking to connect the two vocabulary words into the concept of a command that she should follow (multitasking not being one of her strengths), well that would have been perfectly "normal" for a two-year-old who had Down syndrome.

So, was she acting like a kid who has Down syndrome, or was she just acting like a two-year-old?

Either way, I gave her another chance to respond.

"Fern, come with mama," I said.

Fern stopped and turned around to face me. I smiled, thinking she might come with me, but she gave a little giggle and turned again to continue in the opposite direction. Did I detect a hint of "make me" in that giggle?

I had been warned by other mothers that kids with Down syndrome tended to be runners, and now I wondered whether Fern, who only learned to walk a couple of weeks ago, was showing signs of being a runner. Will has said that sometimes I'm so blinded by the Down syndrome filter I can't see things for what they are. Or, more specifically, I can't see Fern for who she is. I've said that he was so ignorant of the Down syndrome filter, he often misses the obvious. For Fern's sake, I like to think we balance each other out.

"Fern. Come."

Like all kids, whether they have Down syndrome or not, Fern's comprehension outpaced her verbal expression. Fern is unique, however, in that unlike other kids with Down syndrome, Fern has actually been talking, not just signing or grunting, since she was 15 months old. We modeled sign language to bridge the gap between her cognitive and verbal expression, but Fern has been intent on using her voice from the very beginning. If she had wanted to, she could have answered my command with the hilariously exaggerate "NO!" she used when I asked if she wanted to take a bath.

Instead, she just toddled away, and I was left to puzzle it out.

"Okay, Fern," I said, using a trick that always worked with the boys, "mommy is going to walk this way. You can keep going that way, but mommy is going this way."

I turned the corner and entered the next aisle, whistling nonchalantly as I walked to give her an audible clue as to where I was.

At this point, the boys were at a developmental stage where their need to know mommy was present trumped the need to be defiant, and they would come wandering down the aisle and around the corner in search of their whistling mother. This parenting style is proving to be a little trickier with Fern. She is less coordinated, harder to read, slower to process, more easily distracted and independent as hell. I could not be 100 percent certain Fern understood that when I walked away and moved out of sight I did not intend to return to get her. In fact, I'm not even sure she completely understood that I was still in the building, just around the corner, whistling. Object permanence developed later in Fern, and I was not sure how well developed it was even at two-years-old.

I slowed my pace to give Fern a chance to make up her mind. I pretended to look at spaghetti sauce on the end cap a little longer than I needed so she could find me. Still no Fern. This experiment had gone on longer than I would have allowed for either of the boys. I poked my head around the corner to see that Fern was more or less where I had left her, reordering the Asian noodles on the bottom shelf.

I walked back to her and said, "No no, Fern. It's time to go. We have more shopping to do. I am walking this way. You can either walk with me or I will carry you." I offered her my hand. Fern gave no outward sign that she understood me. She simply stood there. Was she listening? Waiting? Processing? Making herself invisible?

I squatted down to be eye-to-eye. "Fern, it is a privilege to be allowed to walk. If you don't walk with me, you will lose that privilege and be required to ride in the cart. Take mama's hand."

There was no perceptible movement in Fern as she kept looking ahead. Even her wispy pigtails seemed frozen in place. I waited a little longer than I might have for the boys, gave her an extra moment to make up her mind. Then, just as I was about to scoop her up to put her in the cart, understanding dawned and Fern slowly reached up and offered her hand. When I took it, she looked up at me and beamed. Together, we walked to the next aisle where I'd left the cart. I whistled. We were making progress.

TWENTY-SEVEN

Popsicles

On a hot summer day, I called out to my kids playing in the courtyard, "Who wants a Popsicle?!" Cypress answered, "I do!" Sylvan said, "Me do!" and Fern said, "Meh!"

Challenge #1: What, exactly, does Fern understand? Does Fern understand that there are Popsicles in her future, or is she just mimicking her brothers?

I went to the freezer and discovered that there were only two Popsicles left. Sylvan and Cypress were already on my heels, but Fern was still making her way up the steps to the kitchen.

"Hmmmm, there are only two Popsicles left."

"I want one!" and "Me too!" rang out.

Challenge #2: Who is getting a Popsicle and who is not? I won't lie. It is tempting to take advantage of Fern's developmental delays. I could slip the boys their Popsicles and distract Fern with the last of the sorbet I've spotted on the side door. I could send the boys out on the deck with their Popsicles and keep Fern with me, maybe offering her a cookie instead so I don't feel bad. Before you condemn me, it would be similar to letting a three-year-old choose whether the family is having hot dogs or pizza for lunch because his one year-old sibling doesn't yet have an opinion.

Except, Fern DOES have an opinion. I've made sure of that. Fern is no pushover. She may not be expressing herself and her opinions in the same way as her twin, but she understands far more than she expresses. By showing up in the kitchen, Fern is showing me she understands that something exciting is happening, and she wants a piece of this freezer action.

Challenge #3: How do I want my kids to interact as siblings? If the boys see me pulling the wool over Fern's eyes, don't you think they'll learn to do that themselves. I can't let my parenting message be, "I'm counting on your cognitive delays to make this parenting dilemma easier" or, "There are only two Popsicles and the boys want them. You may have sorbet, because you are a second class citizen in this family." Or, "You aren't capable of making or deserving of choices. I will make decisions for you."

Do you think I'm over thinking this? This little example of the Popsicle is just one of a thousand scenarios I parent through every day.

Here's what actually happened.

Once Fern joined us in the kitchen I said, "Okay gang, we have two Popsicles and three kids. Who gets a Popsicle?"

"I do!" "Me do!" "Meh!"

"Well, that's not going to work. We need to figure out how to share because there's not enough for everyone to have one."

The boys had already established their preference for Popsicles, but I still wasn't sure Fern knew what was at stake. I picked up a Popsicle and the container of sorbet and held them out to Fern. "Fern, do you want a Popsicle or sorbet?"

She hit the Popsicle, "dat!" Okay. She definitely understands we're talking about Popsicles and she definitely wants one.

This is like negotiating a peace treaty.

"How about I put all the sorbet in one bowl and the Popsicles on a plate? Then we can all have spoons and we can take turns holding the Popsicles."

"No, I want my own," Cypress said.

"Well, who should get the other Popsicle?"

"Sylvan."

"And who should get the sorbet?"

"Fern."

"What if Fern doesn't want sorbet?"

Cypress bent down and got in Fern's face. "Ferny, you can have sorbet. Okay?"

This wasn't Cypress taking advantage of Fern's disability. This was him pressing his advantage of being older.

"Cypress, I'd prefer she have a choice. She wants a Popsicle too. How else can we let everyone have Popsicles?"

"I know! I'll hold the Popsicle and give Ferny bites!"

Challenge #4: Despite the inordinate energy I spend showing people "behind the scenes parenting" of a child with Down syndrome, it's really not all about Fern. My three-year-old just came up with a creative idea for sharing highly coveted Popsicle with his sister. I decided to go with that.

"Okay, let's try it," I said.

We went out to the porch and I unwrapped the Popsicles. I handed a Popsicle to Cypress and reminded him that he was sharing with Fern. He gave her the first bite. Sylvan decided it would be good to share his Popsicle too, so he also gave Fern a bite of his Popsicle. Then Cypress and Sylvan tasted each other's Popscicles.

I sat the bowl of sorbet in front of Fern and told her, "That leaves you in charge of the sorbet girlfriend. You need to make sure everyone gets a bite." She seemed pleased to have a spoon and bowl to herself, and when Cypress got in her face and said, "Ferny, can I have a bite?" she obliged.

TWENTY-EIGHT

The R-Word

About three months ago, I called up my friend Marshall to see how he was doing. He owns several rental properties in my town and was just returning from a long trip away. Our conversation turned quickly to a rant about his negligent tenants.

"One of the retards forgot to fill the oil tank and when the heat stopped working they just left, moved out to stay with their folks. Fuckers. Every goddamn pipe in the place burst!"

Now why did he have to go and use *that* word?

"Know when I heard about it?" I held the phone away from my ear as Marshall's voice went up a decibel. "Yesterday! I went around collecting rent and they informed me that they would not be paying their fucking rent because of the water damage done to their belongings. I'm like, 'What fucking water damage?' and they're like, 'Dude, didn't we tell you the pipes burst?'"

"Oh dear," I said, a little worried by his anger.

"Fuckers. Turns out they had come back to the apartment to get some more clothes and noticed water standing in the kitchen. I'm telling you, these people are so goddamned retarded I wonder how they get through the day."

"Um, yeah, sounds like it," I said uncertainly. Marshall was just venting, and I knew this probably wasn't the time for me to point out to my friend that he needs to clean up his language, but it's in my job description to do so. "Listen, uh, you're not really supposed to use that word anymore."

"What? Fuckers?"

"No, no," I said, "Say fuckers all you want. It's the r-word you're not supposed to use anymore."

"R-word? What the fuck is that?"

"Retarded."

"Well why the hell not?" he asked, turning his fury on me.

"Because of Fern," I explained simply.

"Hmph. Fern's not retarded!" His fury was channeled into something a bit more like passion on this point. He loves my baby girl Fern, who has Down syndrome, and he does not want to hear anyone refer to her as retarded.

"Well, people with intellectual disabilities were called retarded, and now it is used as a diss. And that's not okay." This wasn't the first time I had to explain this point. Ever since Fern was born I've found myself in the uncomfortable role of "advocate" on numerous occasions. It is not a role I enjoy, but with practice it is coming more naturally.

"Shit. Fern can't help the way she is. She was born that way. Now my tenants, *those* people are seriously retarded."

"Listen," I said, "When you call someone retarded, you are saying that they are less intelligent than you and that they are beneath you in some way."

"You're damn straight I am!"

I sucked in my breath. Why can't it just be enough that I am asking him to stop using that word? Can't he just humor me?

"What I'm trying to say is that it is not okay to use Fern's intellectual disabilities as a benchmark for what sucks in this world."

"Shit. You know what I mean. It's just words."

Sometimes I wonder why we are even friends.

To me and Fern, it's not just words. Even when the r-word is not directed at Fern, hearing it used to describe something as defective reminds us that some people believe Fern's disability makes her less of a person, an object of scorn.

There was no point in arguing. My friend was in a mood and he is also the kind of person who is never wrong. So, I let it go.

We ended our call with a promise to get together soon, and I hung up feeling a little stung.

Why couldn't that conversation have gone more like the one I just had with my neighbor?

We were talking over the fence, discussing the new firehouse that was going to be built. When I told him that the alley running between our houses was where they were thinking of building the exit for the fire trucks, he exclaimed, "But that's retarded!"

In response, I lowered my voice and gestured with my head towards Fern, who was playing in the grass a few feet away and said, "I agree, but you're not allowed to use that word anymore."

He caught on quickly and said, "Oh! My bad!"

"It's okay," I said, "I didn't know either."

Then he picked up the conversation and said, "Well, that's a SILLY place for the new road! Silly silly borough!"

I was raised in Floridian culture where using words like "nigger" and "wetback" was part of the norm. Or so I thought. It wasn't until I was a teenager that someone taught me how hurtful those words, and their accompanying sentiments, could be. I had to un-learn what I had been taught. When I chose to make the effort to incorporate "African-American" and "Hispanic" into my own vocabulary, it felt awkward and cumbersome.

Newly enlightened and trying hard to change my own ways, I never had the courage to challenge the bigoted utterances of people, though I inwardly cringed every time I heard them. It shames me to think of how I was a coward.

Nothing like becoming the mother of a child with special needs to make you fearless. I don't let the r-word slip past me.

Upon asking people to refrain from using the r-word, I have been told, "I'm not from America, so I don't have to be politically correct." And, "Retard means to slow something down, and these people are S-L-O-W." And, "There's no point in being offended. You can't teach old dogs new tricks."

Of course, old dogs do learn new tricks. I was almost forty when Fern was born. One day I was chatting with another mother of a baby with Down syndrome, complaining about something, and I said, "Well how retarded is that?" Then it hit me that this little word I had been using to describe just about any situation that pissed me off no longer had a place in my vocabulary. I gave her a guilty look. "I guess we're not supposed to say that anymore." She shrugged and said, "Yeah, guess not."

Unlearning a speech habit and releasing a belief system is hard work. I understood Marshall's resistance and admired my neighbor's willingness.

I talked with Marshall again this week. We had the usual conversation about the weather and our kids, plans for the weekend and the possibility of him stopping by on his way through town. Knowing I was walking right into a tangle of thorns, I braced myself and asked whether anything interesting had happened with his tenants lately.

"Jesus," he said with a deep, irritated sigh, "It's always something with these fucking re…,er, um, idiots."

TWENTY-NINE

Grief

When you first get your child's diagnosis, a lot of people rush in to tell you that your child with special needs will make you a better person. I still struggle with a lot of my shortcomings, but one area that has greatly benefited from the presence of Fern in my life is my ability to feel and express compassion for others.

Without a grief-o-meter, we really have no way of knowing how a person may be experiencing a situation. The pain we suffer is known only to us, and we cannot measure, quantify or compare our experience to another person's. There may be mitigating forces, like a strong faith in God or a comforting family, that make a situation more bearable for some. Or there may be extenuating forces, like a dysfunctional marriage or a lack of resources for recovery, which would make the same situation all but impossible for another. So it's no good trying to decide who suffers more or whether one experience of grief is more valid than another.

When the doctor confirmed what I already suspected, that my newborn baby girl had Down syndrome, I was distraught. Having a child with special needs was the last thing I wanted. I grieved not only for the loss of my "normal" little girl, but also for my happiness, which I assumed was forever dead to me.

Life would never be the same. All hope was lost.

Looking back, in the face of "real" tragedies, I guess it might seem a little self-centered, or perhaps excessive, to have grieved so deeply just because my baby girl was different from what I was expecting. A child was born with an extra chromosome. It happens. Meanwhile, every day mothers all over the world helplessly watch as their children die in horrible circumstances. From poverty and starvation. From senseless acts of war. In freak accidents and by suicide.

I have asked myself, "Who was I to grieve so deeply when nothing was actually lost on the day Fern was born?" No one died. I still had three children to love. Other than having Down syndrome, Fern was basically healthy and she was literally receiving the best care modern medicine had to offer. We were safe and ultimately wanted for nothing. Once we were discharged from the hospital, we would return to our suburban life with ample resources to live comfortably ever after.

Still, I grieved.

And moreover, I have had the audacity to try to offer some measure of comfort to my friends who also grieve. Even in situations I have no way of really understanding, I still believe I have insight on the pain grieving exacts.

Like the time my favorite hygienist was catching me up on the last six months of her life.

"Well," she began, "our vacation didn't go as planned because I ended up in the hospital with crushing pain in my abdomen."

"Welly? Wah?" I asked with my mouth wide opened.

"It turns out I had a four foot section of intestines that had died and become blocked."

"Whaaah? Dats crazah!" I said in disbelief. Up until that day, my hygienist had been the poster child for good health who, from years of conscious eating and routine exercise, exuded glowing energy. We regularly exchanged our favorite smoothie recipes and exercise routines.

"How 'bout it? Spit."

I spat. "How are you feeling?"

"Pretty good," she shrugged, "I'm better now. I just have to watch what I eat. Open wide."

I put my hand up to block her work so I could speak clearly. "No, I mean how are you *feeling?*" Then I laid back and opened wide.

"Oh, that kind of feeling," she said. "Well, to be honest, I'm kind of depressed about it."

I understood this perfectly. My identity as a spectacularly competent mother and in-charge kind of gal was challenged when I gave birth to a child who has special needs. As I reeled from the shock of Fern having Down syndrome, I no longer knew who I was. It was as if a magnetic field of uncertainty had encircled me and the compass I had been using to navigate life was suddenly useless. I was disoriented and lost.

I signaled I wanted to talk and she stopped, hands suspended in front of my face, forefingers looped with silver dental thread. I looked in her earnest eyes and said, "I know what it is to have to redefine myself in a world where nothing I believed about myself seemed true anymore. It's hard."

"Yeah," she nodded, remembering my shock over Fern's diagnosis. "I never saw this coming."

We commiserated, and even laughed, over the loss of our runaway identities and the self-confidence they took with them. In other words, even though there are far worse tragedies than having to redefine who you are in the world, we shared our experience of grief.

Another time, I was arranging my yoga mat for class when I overheard the instructor ask a fellow yoga student whether her much-anticipated grandbaby had been born. A heavy silence followed and I looked up to see the woman was crying and shaking her head.

"No?" asked the instructor.

"There is no grandbaby," the student responded.

I understood her meaning immediately, but our instructor didn't. "Oh. I thought you went to Pittsburgh to help your daughter."

The student nodded, but continued to cry.

"So is the baby late?"

The student gave another shake of her head and our instructor waited.

"The baby didn't make it," the student said in a low, sad voice.

Understanding flooded our teacher's face. "Oh, I'm so sorry," she said, and stood to embrace the student.

It really wasn't any of my business, and it really had nothing to do with anything I had experienced with Fern. But Fern was only a few months old and the tear in my heart was still tender. I got off my mat and met the student where she was selecting props.

"Listen," I said. "I couldn't help but overhear what you just said." She nodded and looked at me through bleary eyes. "I just wanted to say that I'm sorry."

"Thank you," she said, fresh tears filling her eyes.

I went on, "I know it probably seems unrelated, but I just had a baby a few months ago who surprised us by having Down syndrome."

"Oh, the poor thing," she responded, not pityingly but in a way that suggested she had a whole new appreciation for how vulnerable our little babies are in this cruel world.

"Well, it's okay now. But I wanted to say that I know a little of what you are going through right now. It's so horrible when months of anticipation collide with an unexpected and disappointing outcome."

I shared my own taste of disappointment with her, how instead of celebrating Fern's birth, I doubled over crying in disbelief. When I said, "I am so sorry for your loss," she replied, "And I am sorry things didn't turn out the way you'd thought they would."

She graciously allowed my experience of grief, so different from her own, and she allowed me to witness her own. In doing so, we both felt a little better.

Let's face it: No one has the corner on the grief market. There is no scarcity of grief, no black market dealer divvying up a precious commodity to the highest bidder, in this case the person who can offer up the most tear-jerking story. You might say we are all, each of us, entitled to grieve, as much and as often as we need.

Gradually, as I started to understand that life with Fern was going to be delightful, my grief began to ebb and, in its place, feelings of guilt began to grow. Why, exactly, had I experienced so much grief? Was that really grief, or was I just throwing a tantrum because life hadn't turned out the way I'd expected? And had I taken a little too much latitude with my own experience by reaching out to women who had experienced "real" losses, losses I considered worse than my own? After all, I was falling deeply in love with Fern. Maybe it had been presumptuous of me to draw a parallel between my own experience and another person's mourning?

Then one of my closest friends announced that she was getting a divorce.

"Why didn't you tell me things were so bad?" I asked.

"Because it's embarrassing," she said.

"Have you told your co-workers yet?"

"No, I'm not really sure I want to. What will they think of me?"

This hit home for me.

In the days following Fern's birth, the shame I felt made me uncertain about sharing the news with others. At the heart of it, I was hesitant to tell people about Fern having Down syndrome because I wasn't sure how we would be treated. Would people reject me and my baby because our lives weren't perfect and squeaky clean? Blame me for waiting until I was almost 40 to have children? Fault me for choosing prenatal care that led to Fern's diagnosis being a surprise? God, would they pity me?

"I just feel so vulnerable right now," she said.

"Yeah," I agreed, "the last thing you need is to be unpleasantly surprised by people you *think* are your friends."

Fear of rejection, blame and pity is like compost feeding the invasive weed of grief. The need to defend oneself in the face of adversity is cause for grief in and of itself.

I told her, "I also remember questioning my ability to make good decisions after Fern was born. Because if I screwed up something as important as prenatal care, what else was I screwing up?"

"Yes!" she said. "I picked the wrong guy, and I was certain he was Mr. Right. But now it seems like everyone else saw this coming years ago. What's wrong with me?"

Of course, nothing is wrong with either of us. We made some bad decisions, but we were both trying our best. Bad things happen, and sometimes the results are gut-wrenchingly sad.

In the years since Fern was born, I have come to believe that grief, like love and beauty, is both subjective and limitless. I have grieved with cancer patients and survivors, widows and widowers, infertile couples, bankrupt business owners, failed academics and bereaved communities. Each time I hear a story of loss, it awakens in me the memory of my own grief and I usually don't hesitate to reach out. Why? Because in the days after we announced Fern's diagnosis to our friends, it wasn't the clichés and sappy (but often shallow) things people said that bothered me. It was that some people were saying nothing at all.

Still, when my neighbor's teenage son died in a horrible accident, I was reluctant to share my story with her. I did not know her son, but in my book there can be no greater tragedy than burying your own child. Sad as I felt in the days after Fern was born, I simply could not relate to the idea of losing a child you've invested so much of yourself in.

Then as I was falling asleep one night, I remembered the first morning I awoke as "Mother to Fern, the baby with Down syndrome." And while I can't possibly understand what it is to bury a teenage son, I could guess at what those first mornings of awakening as "the Bereaved Mother of Jonas" were like for my neighbor as she endured wave after relentless wave of crushing sadness, reality sinking in even as her mind resisted the truth.

Being Fern's mom has taught me that life is too short for self-doubt and the constant filtering of our emotions. Although I would have done just about anything to renounce my membership to the Grievers Club of America when it was bestowed on me, I now see that there are privileges reserved for those of us who have suffered at the hands of a sometimes cruel and brutal world. Our varied experiences lend certain legitimacy to our unspoken code, which is, "When I see you grieve, I grieve with you." So I summoned the nerve to reach out to her and shared my small morning story via a private message on Facebook.

"Hey Claire, You were the last thing on my mind when I went to bed last night, and the first thing I thought of when I woke up. It's a bit presumptuous of me to suggest I know anything of your grief, but I do remember how awful it was to learn of Fern's diagnosis and to grieve for the little girl I'd never have. The day of her diagnosis was bad enough, with lots of tears. But there were so many things that had to be done, I spent the day crying and a little distracted. The very worst moment for me was in the quiet early hours of the next morning. There was just a brief second after I woke up when I believed that maybe, just maybe, it was all a nightmare and that I would get out of bed and still be pregnant with two healthy babies.

The moment when I realized that it was all true, that my life had forever changed, was the lowest point in my life."

Within a few hours Claire had responded.

"Thank you Heather. I had the same thing happen to me the other day. You awake thinking what a horrible nightmare, and reality crashes down upon you. You wonder how can a person live with is much pain/heartache. I know this happens every day and people move on, but right now I just don't know how."

Even though everyone would agree that losing a child is far worse than learning your child has Down syndrome, my neighbor graciously accepted my willingness to grieve with her and took it for what it was: a humble offer of friendship.

Anyone who has experienced a major life event knows this strange circumstance where, at a time when you need support, the very people who are there to support you sometimes also need you to play a certain role for them. For some, we were the recipients of someone paying forward a kindness they had received in their own times of troubles. For others, Fern presented an opportunity to prove to themselves that they had it in them to love a child like Fern. The most memorable visits I had, though, were from people who were still healing from their own previous hurts. In the days after we announced that Fern had Down syndrome, close friends as well as women I barely knew told me their stories of loss. It didn't matter to me that these women did not know *exactly* what I was going through. All that mattered to me was that they were willing to hold up their own imperfect lives for me to see, mirroring my pain back to me, validating my experience of grief without judging me, healing me even as they healed themselves.

Perhaps our seemingly unrelated experiences have taught us all the same lesson: Grieving is not a contest. If it were, no one in their right mind would want to win.

To my relief, almost everyone in our community responded to Fern's birth and diagnosis with love and acceptance, and it wasn't long before I got back on my feet again. My journey from feeling isolated to feeling flooded with gratitude was made speedier by everyone who reminded me that I was not alone, who witnessed but did not wallow in my pain, who shared their stories and listened to mine, and who, importantly, refrained from telling me everything was going to be okay. To every neighbor, friend, stranger, and family member who reached out to humbly share their own stories of grief, I am indebted. Part of the healing equation, now, is to pay it forward. Therefore, when I know someone is grieving, no matter how hard or easy I may judge the situation to be, I hope I always have the audacity reach out to *try* to offer that most precious of human connections: compassion.

THIRTY

Perfection

If you had asked me fifteen years ago whether my life plan included having a child with special needs, the answer would have been an emphatic NO! Actually, fifteen years ago someone did ask me to envision what my future would look like, and recently, that memory surprised me.

It was the year 2000 and, with the help of an interpreter, I was negotiating the price of a teapot with a shopkeeper in Xian, China. The teapot was heavy, perhaps made of iron, and about the size of a flat bottomed baseball. It had a perfectly arched handle and a darling little spout with a pouty lip, perfect for catching the last drop of my latest obsession, Jasmine tea.

The dealer wanted $40 for the teapot. I loved it and wanted it badly, and of course my face showed it, but I balked. Working through the interpreter, the shopkeeper came down to $35 and then he wouldn't budge. I am a terrible judge of what things should cost and an even worse negotiator, but I couldn't imagine paying that much for a teapot when I was living comfortably on just $25 per day in the not-yet developing parts of China. So I left the shop without buying the tea pot, and the volunteer interpreter, a girl barely 17 years old, followed right behind me.

We spent another hour walking around the market, not seeing anything close to the teapot I'd already fallen in love with. Reluctantly, I went back to the shop to take another look at the teapot. The shopkeeper was polite, but firm on his price. I didn't know if I was being cheap or frugal, but at only half way through my trip, I didn't think I could afford to break my budget. I turned to leave again when the man stopped me and said, through our surprised interpreter, that he would like to read my palm.

"How much does *that* cost?" I asked suspiciously.

"Nothing," he said, through the interpreter.

"Do you think I can trust him?" I asked the girl.

"I think that it is okay," she said.

So I sat on a stool in front of the man, with our knees almost touching and the girl standing beside us.

Speaking through the girl he said, "Do you have a dream for your future?"

I had to think for a little bit. I was 27 years old and happily single. I had just finished a two-year teaching contract in Japan and, after traveling in China, I would return to Japan to live on an organic farm for a few months. On some level I was entertaining the possibility of becoming a farmer. At the same time, I never wanted the experience of traveling solo in exotic places to end. I had hitch-hiked solo the length of Japan and back and had recently been to Thailand. My day dreams consisted of schemes for making a career of traveling.

I shrugged.

The man asked again, "What is your dream? You must have a dream for the future, yes?" His tone was insistent.

I closed my eyes for a moment and tried to think past the near future, full of hedonistic plots to experience the world, to visualize where I would be in ten or fifteen years. And, with surprisingly little effort, I got it.

I opened my eyes and nodded.

"Okay, open your hand and turn your palm up."

I did as the man asked. Then I watched as he ripped the foil lining out of a pack of cigarettes, spit into it, wadded it up and dropped it into my outstretched palm.

"Now close your hand," the girl seemed very curious as she translated.

I closed my fingers around the spit-wad.

"When the pain becomes too intense, just nod your head."

The girl and I looked at each other. "What??" I asked. She turned back to the man for clarification and then back to me to confirm, "He says that when the pain becomes too much, you need to nod your head."

Nervous, I agreed. Then the man hovered one of his hands about a six inches above my closed fist, and another about six inches below it.

"Close your eyes and think very hard about the dream you have for your life." I raised my eyebrows. He said something in an insistent tone and the girl-woman translated, "He says you need to focus on your dream."

So I closed my eyes and suddenly saw my life's dream very clearly. In it, I was standing in front of a cozy home with a fenced yard. There were pretty flowers in garden beds that someone, my husband, helped me build and, although I couldn't see them, there were children, my children, playing somewhere. It was the American ideal of "home," where everything is perfect. The lawn was trimmed, the children were smart and well-behaved, and the fence was even white picket! And while the imagery was lovely, it was the feel of the place that I remember most. It was the feeling of love and contentment, of knowing my place in the world and being satisfied with it.

I was surprised that something as common as making a home was my life's dream, given all the adventures I had on my to-do list. Certainly that was the first time I had seriously experienced the desire to be a wife and mother, but there was no question in my mind: My dream was to create a perfect and loving home.

Suddenly, I noticed a warm sensation in my palm and within a minute the warmth intensified. The man said something and the girl asked, "Do you feel anything?" I nodded once in agreement. Then the heat turned from very hot to outright burning. I nodded furiously and opened my eyes in time to see that the man had brought his hands to within an inch on either side of my closed fist. I caught the intense look in his eye as he removed his hands and, in an instant, the pain was gone. I opened my palm to find that the spit wad was charred black, and there was a small painful blister the size of an eraser head on my palm.

"Now your dream has been burned into your skin and it will come true."

I laughed. "How did he do that?"

The girl was as amazed as me. Then she said, "He wants you to open your palm again."

I complied. He drew a straight line down my palm. "What is that?" he asked.

I said, "One?"

Then he drew a circle on my palm and raised his eyebrows in question.

"Zero?" I guessed.

He smiled and said, "Yes. Ten. That is how much you should pay me. Ten yen."

I threw back my head and laughed, "Ha ha! No, you said the palm-reading would be free!"

He looked disappointed until I said, "Okay. I will buy that tea pot for $35."

I met William Wise, my future husband and father of my children, just six months later. I always say that Will isn't the man of my dreams because I wasn't smart enough to dream up marrying someone this good. We have a cozy home with a fenced yard and pretty flowers in garden beds we built together. And there, playing next to the book shelf where we keep a small, heavy teapot are our beautiful, smart, (usually) well-behaved children. We are each other's world, and loving the people in this family is as fulfilling as I imagined it would be. I know my place in this family, and while I sometimes feel I got more than I bargained for, I have everything I need. My life is messy, sometimes complicated and often painful, but this life is my dream come true. It's everything I imagined even though it's not at all what I expected. This is what perfect looks like.

.　　　　　.　　　　　.

I wish I could close my eyes and get such a clear vision of Fern's future. Instead of staring hard directly into the future, which only makes it even more impossible to see, I use something akin to averted vision. Possibilities form in the corner of my eye and I can see that Fern will probably learn to read, perhaps even for pleasure. I can see that she will probably have a passion for movement and exercise, perhaps swimming or biking. I can see that she might find a useful way to spend her adult years, either employed or as a volunteer. I can make out the fuzzy figure of a future partner, possibly even a wedding day when we welcome another person with special needs into our family. And friends. I definitely see friends in Fern's future.

Right now, Fern is undeniably adorable and, as every mother knows in times of frustration, it is really to a child's advantage to be cute. But it won't always be unruly pigtails, sticky Popsicles and potty-training, and Fern won't always be cute. We have big challenges ahead of us.

In 1983, when I was wearing Kangaroos and parachute pants, people with Down syndrome had an average life expectancy of 25 years old. Thirty years later, Kangaroos are back in fashion and, thanks to medical advancements and better overall care, people with Down syndrome are given a life expectancy of over 60, and growing. I will be dead by the time Fern is 60, but I can almost guarantee that she will no longer be adorable. She will have aged faster than her twin, she may have Alzheimer's, and she almost certainly will not be living independently. Who will take care of her then?

And there's the bit about us forever being married to the Modern Medical Machine. When Fern was a few months old, an endocrinologist ran a test to determine more specifically why Fern's thyroid levels were low. Either her thyroid was not functioning at optimally or at all, or the body was actually attacking the thyroid, which makes it an autoimmune disorder. Some people have had success managing low thyroid function with diet and exercise, and I was hoping that might be an option for us. However, Fern has the autoimmune variety, and we sure as hell aren't going to treat that with rhubarb and granola.

So, we try to strike a balance: organic vegetables from our garden, DHA's for increasing brain function (because I would give anything for her to be smarter), and lifelong dependence on the Modern Medical Machine for thyroid medicine (and who knows what's to come) to keep her alive. And I'm okay with this. Having Fern has made me less certain about everything, and this has been an immeasurable gift to me. It's as if I can finally relax because I see that absolutely nothing is under control. I am able to hold my convictions a little lighter and use the resources available to me to make life better.

One irony I think about a lot is that in those same 30 years the Modern Medical Machine was developing breakthrough treatments to improve the life quality and life expectancy of people who have Down syndrome, it also developed a simple blood test that is nearly 100% accurate in determining whether a baby will be born with Down syndrome. And I wonder whether the rate of aborting children with chromosomal abnormalities will increase.

I remain unabashedly pro-choice, but if you don't really know anything about having a kid with Down syndrome, choice in the matter is an illusion. That's partly why I wrote this book. We live in an era when it's not unusual for women to receive a prenatal diagnosis that starts with an apology and ends with an invitation. "I'm sorry. The test indicates a high risk of the fetus having Down syndrome. Would you like to schedule an appointment to terminate the pregnancy?" The assumption is that if a child is not "perfect," it is not wanted.

A friend, who is 41, just had a pregnancy scare and she confided to me that she was worried that on top of having an unplanned baby, that baby might also have special needs. As the mother of a child with special needs, I was not offended. Instead, I felt like I was in a place to say, "I really hope your child does not have special needs."

I love Fern, and I am thankful for all of the personal growth that I have done as a result of having this eye-opening, heart-opening experience. But in no way would I ever begrudge someone for being relieved their child does not have an extra chromosome, especially if it is someone who is close to us. Our friends and family have more education than the average person on the subject of "What it Means to be a Parent of a Child with Special Needs." People who are close to our family watched how painful it was to hand Fern over for heart surgery at just four months old, how we struggled to breastfeed, and how we will always wait and wait for every milestone. If we were to conceive another child, I would very much be relieved if the prenatal tests showed that it did not have an extra chromosome.

But if the baby did happen to have an extra chromosome, I would not choose abortion.

I would never minimize the seriousness of what lay ahead of parents who decide to keep a baby who will be born with Down syndrome. While having a child with special needs was not a matter of life or death for me in the way that, say, having open-heart surgery was for Fern, it did dramatically change my life as I knew it. It was the death of a life that I liked pretty well. Parenting a child with special needs can be a hard road and I understand if you don't think you're up for the challenge. I'm sure I didn't feel up to the challenge when I first learned of Fern's diagnosis. But if you are making the choice to abort a child strictly out of fear, then I think you might be underestimating yourself and putting a little too much stock into what other people have told you a good life should look like. Sometimes we need to lean into the hard and accept it as a gift. Often it is the hard stuff that makes life so rich and deeply rewarding.

Here's the thing a lot of parents of kids who have special needs will tell you: although the emotional and mental growth required of me was difficult and painful and sometimes even felt unbearable, I never want my old life back. Having Fern is one of the best things that ever happened to me, even if having Down syndrome isn't the best thing to have happen to her. She helped me understand the gift of shared vulnerability and brought out the best in our community. I wish I was the kind of person for whom compassion and patience came more naturally, that I could have embraced the value of people who have special needs without Fern having Down syndrome. But mine was a rigid heart and Fern was the perfect baby to soften it.

When we received Fern's diagnosis, I thought we were being shackled to a ball and chain that would weigh us down for the rest of our lives. Instead, Fern freed me of my narrow world-view and also from the burden of trying to find my place in it. Cypress, Sylvan, and especially Fern solidified my place in this world. As their mom, my job is to provide a loving home, nurture their passions and hopefully pass along enough wisdom so that they can make their own dreams come true.

Whenever someone says, "Fern knew what she was doing when she chose you as a mom," I just roll my eyes. I don't believe there are little souls up there picking and choosing which woman's womb they are going to occupy or which father's life they are going to upend. To me, it's just biology, cell division and luck. But on one sappy point, I do have to agree: just as Fern was the perfect baby for me, I am the perfect mom for Fern. I believe in her and I know she will go far. I can imagine a day in the not-too-distant-future when I sit knee to knee with Fern and ask her, "What is your dream for your life?" Already, I know that Fern is growing up to be the kind of woman who will have an answer to this question and, as flawed an individual as I am, I am the perfect person to help her achieve that dream.

As much as the future scares me sometimes, I am excited to see Fern come into her Fern-iness as she grows to know her own mind and listen to her own heart. Having a child with special needs isn't turning out to be the nightmare I was dreading. Quite the opposite. Fern plays a starring role in my life's dream come true. Our happiness isn't remarkable. In fact, it is as they say, "garden variety." Picked at peak perfection, it is sweet, a little blemished and unmistakably good. This life might not be *exactly* what I envisioned for myself, but I when I was dreaming up my best life, I did not have the wisdom to know that the last thing I wanted would be exactly what I needed.

Made in the USA
Charleston, SC
21 February 2017